Presented To:

_____

From:

_____

Date:

_____

IT'S YOUR TIME

Your Generation Awaits You

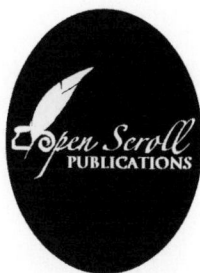

Open Scroll
PUBLICATIONS

IT'S YOUR TIME

Your Generation Awaits You

MICHAEL EKWULUGO

Published by Open Scroll Publications

Copyright © 2014 by Michael Ekwulugo

First published 2014 by Open Scroll Publications Ltd,
25 Mary Street, Jewellery Quarter,
Birmingham, B3 1UD.

ISBN 978-0-9930876-0-8

A CIP catalogue record of this book is available from the British Library.

First Edition.

Cover design and Typeset by Open Scroll Publications.

Printed in Great Britain.

To all the underdogs out there who have never found the courage to bark ... your bite will make up for lost time!

IF I ATTEMPTED to list all the people who have helped make this dream come true, I'd have to write another book! I've been blessed with so many beautiful people in my life.

So I'll attempt to keep it brief.

Mum: You are a special human being. As a parent, you are award-winning. As a mentor you are second to none; and as a ministry/prayer partner, you pack a punch lady! I love you more than okro soup and gari. You are the most dynamic person that I know, and I'm eternally grateful for the privilege of being your son.

Dad: Thank you for refusing to join those secret Lodges in the 70s. You stood firm for Christ when others were bowing away in Babylon. You've always loved the Lord ... and for that, you deserve a standing ovation.

Katrina: My lady, my lover, my wife. You were one of the biggest inspirations behind this book. I'm in awe of the woman you've become. That's why I fought so hard to get you on the front cover. You are the poster child for what God can do with a surrendered life. As a wife you're indispensable; as a mother you're unequalled; and as an adviser, you're a game-changer. I need you to know how precious you are to me. My life turned around the day that I met you ... *thank you for always believing in me.*

Joshua: You are a 21st-century warrior. I already see the man that you are. When I look at you, I see the 'upgrade' of myself. Thank you for your love, support, and patience during the writing of this book. Now that it's finished, I'm going to 'school' you at FIFA!

Tanta (Nathaniel): You are the kindest and most gentle soul I know. Thank you for always putting others first ... you are a king in the making. Your name means God's gift, and that's exactly what you are. You are a gift to your generation. Just keep being *you* son — you are quietly formidable!

Dee: You're a literary legend! You're such a gifted and prolific writer. Yours is a hard act to follow girl ... *but I'm trying!* Thank you for your endless encouragement — it means so much. Thank you for proof reading this volume so quickly. You were the first person to read this book, and your constructive comments gave me the courage to publish it.

Nigel: Bro-in-law thank you for my office conversion: it does exactly what it says on the box! That place was built to bless. Each time I enter it, I smile and think of you. Chineke gozie gi Ooooo!

Bindi (Raj): You are royalty. You are a true-to-life Esther and I'm in awe of the relationship you've built with your heavenly Father. You are truly heaven's own. Mohammed Ali may have floated like a butterfly and stung like a bee, but you look like a lamb and live like a lion (Proverbs 28:1). High five Sis!

Dre (Andre): You are a lion tamer (just as well being married to Raj eh?) Andre you are the perfect paradox: a Yardie gentleman! You are pure class mate, and your Bible-bearing skills are epic! Thank you for being the little brother I never had. You are a true prince of God.

Aunty Ann (Angel): What can I say Aunty? How many people are blessed enough to have a tangible angel watching over them? Your presence in my life was God's design. You are one of God's greatest exhibitions of grace on this earth. I bless the lord for your life!

Jason: Yes bro ... the Blues just got Mo' better! Thank you for being my dream-keeper. You are the most faithful friend I could have ever asked for. Your unconditional love has been a staple in this journey: *thank you Jay.*

Jack-attack (Jackie): Thank you for letting Jason give me asylum in your home in the 90s, when I was a spiritual refugee in my own personal war: *World War Me.*

O'neil & Jo: Neily, you are Jamaica's most prestigious export. Your friendship and prayer-partnership over the years have helped me access heaven at some of the toughest times of my pastoral journey. I can think of no other general that I'd rather be on the battlefield with than you. Thank you.

Jo, you are the most multi-talented person I know ... is there *anything* you can't do? Thank you for being such a pillar in my life, you're the akee to Neily's saltfish: together you're such a 'kingdom dish'!

Paul & Rachel: Paul, you are integrity personified. You have restored my confidence in Christian virtues. Thank you for always having my back, and for always being a true ambassador of Christ.

Rachel, you are one of the most unassuming creative geniuses I know. Thank you for always being such a blessing. You are heaven's most faithful courier. Thank you for surrounding us with your Spirit-filled works of art.

Angelina: Ange, you are a walking bless pot! Thank you for always *representin'!* You never shy away from a challenge, and you never turn your back on a genuine need. You're a truly amazing sister-in-law and friend.

Lady Di, Mr T, Mikey T: You guys are as much family to me as you are to Katrina. Thank you for always loving and supporting me over the years — I love you all.

Trevor Jr (NewStyle Radio): Thank you for your support over the years bro, who would have thought we'd still be tag-teaming on the radio 12 years later? Keep blessing the city Trev!

Robin, Mexy, and Joylyn (My Technical Consultants): Collectively, you guys are like the 'Q' to my 007. Thank you for your technical expertise, and for always making time for me.

My Faithful TLC Family: You guys are right out of the 'Upper Room'! Thank you for bearing the DNA of Christ. You are the most beautiful, loving, and sincere church family that I've ever had the honour of serving. Thank you for your love, support, and faithful prayers.

My Bishops: A massive thank you to all the veterans of the Glory Summit in Nigeria. The Lord has used each of you to mentor me from afar over the years. Bishop Goddy Okafor, Bishop Zilly Aggrey, Bishop Emmah Isong, Bishop Humphrey Erumaka, Bishop Chidi Okorafor, Dr Paul Enerche, Bishop Henry Nathaniel, and Bishop Joshua Telina, you have all played an inestimable role in providing me with the right 'tools' for ministry. You are God's modern-day generals — and I salute you all.

Holy Spirit: You are my teacher, my counsellor and my friend. Your faithful presence in my life is the air that I breath. Other writers speak of a muse; I can only speak of the miracle of your still, small voice ... *thank you for being my inspiration!*

PART III:
The Unleashing – Stepping Out On Purpose

THE FORCE IS WITH YOU

Our deepest fear is not that we are inadequate. Our deepest fear is that we are powerful beyond measure. It is our light, not our darkness that most frightens us.

— Marianne Williamson

RECENTLY, A POWERFUL and potent force has begun to rumble deep down on the inside of you. A godly force. One that is becoming increasingly difficult to suppress or ignore. Like a sleeping volcano that has suddenly begun to stir, these strange feelings seem to be intensifying with time. They keep threatening to erupt and spill out into every area of your nice, tidy, uneventful life.

I must warn you right from the start: you are never going to break free from this force. This force is a gift. It was something embedded into the core of your being to immunise you against settling for less in life. It's something that inoculates you against those toxic little feelings of inadequacy that sometimes try to settle over you. The force that I'm talking about is the power of your God-given purpose:

> *But we have this treasure in earthen vessels, that the*
> *excellence of the power may be of God and not of us.*
> — 2 Corinthians 4:7 NKJV

Now if you're anything like me, then you've probably spent so much time admiring, and being in awe of other peoples' gifts and abilities, that you've barely had time to appreciate (let alone celebrate) your own. And whilst it's an admirable quality to esteem and celebrate others, failing to recognise the gift that *you* are to your generation, would be an absolute travesty! That is why I had to put pen to paper.

Dear friend, you are a wonderfully sophisticated tool in the hand of a very creative God. Be assured of this one thing: in these dark times characterized by hopelessness and pain, you're here to make a difference. You're here to help unhinge the forces of darkness raging against your family, community, and wider sphere of influence.

Let the following scripture serve as a launch pad for the journey you and I are about to begin:

> *You will be a new threshing instrument with many sharp teeth. You will tear your enemies apart, making chaff of mountains.*
>
> — Isaiah 41:15 NLT

STRAIGHT TALK

I wish that someone had been able to place this book in my hand twenty years ago. During those terrible times that I spent wallowing away in the concentration camps of unseen enemies, oblivious to my birthright blessings as a child of God. This volume would have saved me so much time and spared me so many years of needless anguish. Whoever said ignorance is bliss, lied!

Ignorance is one of the quickest roads to ruin. When you are ignorant about what God says concerning you, agents of darkness will heckle and torment you. Unscrupulous individuals will manipulate and abuse you. History attests that the prince of darkness is happiest when operating covertly behind the scenes of our lives. He relishes the kind of free-and-easy access given to him (and his minions) by that infamous cloak of mind-darkness: ignorance.

The Bible warns:

> *... my people have gone into captivity, because they have no knowledge ...*
> — Isaiah 5:13 NKJV

> *My people are destroyed for lack of knowledge ...*
> — Hosea 4:6 NKJV

So, my purpose in writing this book was to give you (the reader) something that I now deem more precious than gold: instructions on how to become a first-class you — rather than a second-class someone else. I'm exited that you've picked up this book, **but be warned**: *every ceiling of limitation that you've ever lived under is about to be smashed to smithereens.*

May your dreams be reignited, and may your eyes be opened to see — perhaps for the first time — how limitless your life was meant to be.

> *... knowledge will rescue the righteous.*
> — Proverbs 11:9b NLT

Let the journey begin!

N.B. Please note that scripture quotations taken from the NLT, TLB, and NKJV Bibles, appear with their original American spellings.

PART I
THE AWAKENING

RECOVERING

LOST

GROUND

Deep calls unto deep ...

Psalms 42:7 NKJV

CHAPTER 1

SAY MY NAME

When someone loves you, the way they say your name is different. You know that your name is safe in their mouth.

— Jess C. Scott, The Intern

I WOULD LIKE TO begin this book with a bold statement: **what you see is most certainly <u>not</u> what you get.** There is so much more to your life than meets the eye.

Tell me, have you ever had the feeling that life was somehow lying to you? Financially you're hardly what anyone would describe as 'loaded' (in fact you may be struggling with debt right now). And yet, deep down, you just can't shake the feeling that one day, you're going to be wealthy!

Perhaps, you recall times in your life, when you received news about one of your peers moving forward in life. Settling down in marriage, starting a family, launching out in business, or embarking upon a life-long ambition. And although a part of you was genuinely pleased for them, the other part of you quickly plummeted into a private panic attack. Before you could catch yourself and process the information properly, a huge flash flood of fear and anxiety swept over you, sending you into a mini crisis.

Mentally you found yourself regressing back in time to a sepia-toned memory. Suddenly you were back in the school playground again, standing amongst a dwindling line-up of sorry-looking hopefuls, desperately trying to get picked for someone's team — *anyone's!*

You see yourself trying to catch the eye of one of the team captains: maybe they'll feel sorry for you and be moved to make a 'mercy pick'. But this doesn't happen. No one picks you, and you end up on one of the teams by default: '*Eeny meenie miny mo*, right then … I guess you're over there mate!'

And as you leap forward as athletically as possible (in a burst of adrenalin-fuelled determination to impress your new team members) you become faintly aware of two formidable forces fighting each other for first place in your psyche: *rejection* and *humiliation*.

Well, that was then — and this is now. And yet at times, it can so often feel as though very little has changed over the years. Different time: yes. Different place: certainly. But as others step forward to join the honourable ranks of 'newly-weds', 'thriving new business owners', 'Parents To Be', 'Possessors Of A University Degree' (or even of that most venerated of all academic accolades: the PhD), we can still feel as though we've been left languishing on life's sidelines.

May I have your undivided attention for a moment? I have an important announcement for you. **Your days of waiting around on the sidelines are over.** Destiny has just called your name!

Perhaps amidst the madcap swirl of activities clamouring for your attention, you didn't quite hear His voice. But listen closely … He's still calling. Just stand still for a moment. Take a deep breath, and just let the crowd thunder past you and fade into the distance …

Now can you hear Destiny's voice? He's trying to whisper something to your heart. Oh, you'll know when you've heard His voice. It's an unmistakable sound. It's a sound that mutes all other voices — especially those poisonous ones. You know, the ones that love to hiss disaster scenarios at you first thing every morning? The ones that mock and snigger at every inspired idea that you've ever had.

No. When Destiny calls your name, a little flame of godly assurance will suddenly flicker into existence in the pit of your stomach. An inexplicable peace will settle over you. Against all logic and common sense, something strange and unprecedented will begin to happen to you: *you'll start believing in yourself!*

Something will begin to rise up from the very core of your being. Something immutable. Something unstoppable. Not a fad. Not a mere feeling. But an irrepressible conviction:

IT IS YOUR TIME!

Not tomorrow. Not when you have all the answers. Not when you feel qualified. And certainly not when everyone around you starts approving of you. But right now!

I have never believed in coincidence — so I won't start now. I don't believe that you've picked this book up by accident. It's in your possession because something momentous is coming your way? A life-altering blessing has been dispatched from heaven for you. This book is simply preparing you for your promotion. This is a season like no other.

But in order to shuttle to those new heights, you're going to need a new kind of momentum — a new kind of focus. This book was designed to do just that.

It will help you 'change lanes', and build the right momentum for lift-off.

So, resolve in your heart not to merely toy with the idea of stepping forward. Just step forward and take your place in history — heaven has just head-hunted you.

> *Do not be afraid, for I have ransomed you. I have*
> *called you by name; you are mine.*
> — Isaiah 43:1b NLT

Points To Ponder ...

- List three personal attributes that have remained with you since childhood. How can you further develop these qualities?
- List three negative characteristics that have plagued you since childhood. How do these flaws affect you now in the present?
- What things (not yet actualized) are you determined to achieve in your lifetime?

Prayer Time

Dear Lord, thank you for new beginnings. Thank you for safeguarding me through the rejections and disappointments of life. I recognise that I still carry traces of hurt from those experiences. Holy Spirit, I turn to you now for help. The Bible teaches that through declarations and a new mindset, I can be healed, and restored (Job 22:28, Romans12:2). So, in obedience to your word, I now declare that:

- *I was chosen and set apart before the foundations of the earth (Ephesians 1:3-4).*

- *I have been divinely hand-picked for a specific assignment and purpose (John 15:16).*

- *This is my time to arise. It is the most fertile, fruitful and prolific period of my life (Psalms 102:13). Amen.*

CHAPTER 2

STAGE FRIGHT

Humility is not thinking less of yourself, it's
thinking of yourself less.

– C. S. Lewis

BUT WHY ME? With over 7 billion people roaming around on this vast planet, why would the Lord single me out? With all of my — how can I put this delicately? — 'issues', why would an all-knowing, all-seeing God, lavish heaven's precious resources on a volatile, unpredictable prospect like me? I mean — while we're 'keeping it real'— with all the bright, beautiful people bustling around on planet earth, how could anything *I* choose to do (or not do) possibly make a difference to anyone?

Like a million boomerangs let loose at once, these relentless questions reverberate in our minds, until we finally checkmate ourselves. We talk ourselves out of every opportunity that comes our way. It's as though we've trained ourselves to live in a septic world where toxic thoughts become the norm, and discouragement is just another part of our daily diets.

But we must rebel. A quiet riot. We must dare to defy these lying voices. Buried beneath these soul-destroying lies (the ones that try to convince us that we're nothing more than a minuscule part of a perishing herd), there rests an undeniable truth.

I have written this book to remind you of that truth.

There is no one quite like you on this earth.

You are one of a kind. You have been strategically placed in this timeline of history for a glamorous and glorious future.

Everything about you is deliberate. Your smile. Your humour. Your passions. Your uniqueness. Even your peculiar set of life experiences, and your unusual catalogue of talents. And what about those weird and wacky perspectives of yours? You know, the ones that keep getting you in trouble with the conventional crowd? All of these wonderfully complex things, combine to form a magnificent, one-off tapestry. You've been designed to capture the attention of your generation.

Nelson Mandela, Mother Teresa, Mahatma Gandhi, Eleanor Roosevelt, Paul the Apostle, Esther, and of course, the greatest of them all: Jesus of Nazareth, were all God's gifts to humanity. They were heaven's treasure on earth. But heaven is still in a generous mood. God is still sprinkling the earth with sparkling characters. And you are one of His latest offerings.

But the real gem of who you are, can often be buried beneath the complexities of your character. Remember that game we used to play as kids: *Pass The Parcel?* Well, that's the way this book was designed to work.

The Points-To-Ponder section at the end of each chapter, gives you the opportunity to discard a layer of pessimism from your thinking. Each chapter allows you to 'bin' some of the mindsets that have been holding you back.

It's crucial that you begin to identify these negative attitudes before they start undermining your confidence at every turn. Left unchecked, these negative mindsets will give you 'stage fright'!

Each time you make a decision to climb onto the podium of your purpose, you'll freeze. You'll hear imaginary hecklers in the audience. Voices from the past crudely belching out reasons why you don't qualify to have a voice in this world. Why you don't deserve to be heard; why no one will ever be interested in your silly, little contributions. So, before we go any further, let's dispel with a few of these lies.

THE GOOD THE BAD AND THE UGLY

For the record, your life isn't an audition! In spite of the catalogue of issues that sometimes plague you (self-doubt, self-condemnation, lack of self-control etc.) nothing that you find yourself grappling with, comes as a surprise to the Lord. According to God's Word, none of these things disqualify you from your calling.

> *For the gifts and the calling of God are irrevocable.*
> — Romans 11:29 NKJV

Like an artist's studio, your life is the Lord's 'creative corner'. There is nothing in your journey that catches Him off guard. He never has to stagger back, and take a few deep breaths in a brown paper bag to compose Himself because of your blunders. God is omniscient. He knows what's coming before it comes! So just let the following scriptures wash over you:

> *O Lord, you have examined my heart and know everything about me.*

You know when I sit or stand. When far away
you know my every thought.

You chart the path ahead of me and tell me where
to stop and rest. Every moment you know where I am.

You know what I am going to say before I even say it.

You both precede and follow me and place your hand
of blessing on my head.

— Psalms 139:1-5 TLB

Also:

You were there while I was being formed in utter seclusion!

You saw me before I was born and scheduled each day
of my life before I began to breathe. **Every day was**
recorded in your book!

— Psalms 139:15-16 (emphasis mine) TLB

Now, imagine watching a movie with a friend who's already seen it. While you frantically bite your nails and try not to fall off the edge of your seat, they can just sit there entertaining themselves — half watching you, and half watching the screen! When the suspense becomes unbearable, and you turn to them and say something like 'OK, just tell me this ONE thing: is she going to die?!?!' They can calmly smile and say, 'All in good time mate … *all in good time!*'

This is what life is like when we learn to walk with the Lord. When we live in His Presence, not only do we get to speak with someone who's already seen the movie, we get to sit behind the scenes with the Writer/Director Himself. We get to watch the action as it unfolds in real time. We become like an actor attending the premier of his latest movie. Instead of having to obsess about shooting hundreds of scenes, he can finally just relax and enjoy the whole film.

> *Declaring the end from the beginning, and from ancient times things that are not yet done ...*
> — Isaiah 46:10 NKJV

AND ACTION!

No wonder why the Lord never panics or loses control. Even when we mess up and miss the mark!

Have you ever wondered why even when you're praying in 'panic mode' about your problems and pressures, there's still always a kind of peace to be found in His presence? It's because the Lord not only knows what's going to happen in the 'movie' of your life, but He also knows how blessed the ending is. I'm reminded here of one of Christ's many titles: The Author and Finisher of our faith (Hebrews 2:12).

When you consider all those colourful biographies in the Bible: Jacob, Rahab, Mary Magdalene et cetera, some of your own off-the-grid experiences suddenly begin to make perfect sense. These biblical biographies are like vivid 3D scenes, signposting you to your own future.

So, as you begin your expedition into your personal promise land, I pray that your spirit will be imbued with a supernatural confidence. I pray that like Joshua and Caleb in the Bible, you will rise up and meet every giant of opposition head on!

> *The wicked flee when no one is chasing them!* **But the godly are bold as lions!**
> —Proverbs 28:1 (emphasis mine) TLB

Points To Ponder ...

- If you could travel back in time and alter any of your life experiences, what would you change?
- Would you be willing to forfeit the lessons learned, and the wisdom gleaned from such tutorial journeys?
- How have these experiences impacted your perspectives in life so far?

Prayer Time

Dear Lord, thank you for the plans that you have for me. I recognise now that everything I've been through (the good, the bad, and the ugly) will make me stronger/wiser in the end (Romans 8:28). Lord I repent of any choices or decisions that I've made which have been harmful to my destiny. In the name of Jesus,

- *I release myself from guilt, regret, and self-doubt (Romans 8:1).*

- *I release myself from every counter-productive attitude hindering my progress in life (1 Corinthians 2:14).*

- *I claim and receive mercy, new opportunities, and fresh streams of inspiration (Lamentations 3:22-23).*

- *I now declare by faith, that I have just stepped into a new era of favour. This is a brand new season in my life (Isaiah 43:18-19) Amen.*

CHAPTER 3

FACING THE GIANTS

Nobody can hurt me without my permission.

– Mahatma Gandhi

FACT: THERE ARE no promise lands without giants. In order to excel and stand out in this life, you'd better be ready for a fight. A good old-fashioned, bare-knuckle 'tear up'! But be warned: the giants that you and I face in the 21st century, aren't exactly your usual 'garden variety'. No, these modern 'Goliaths' are hybrids. Upgrades, with the sickening ability to morph into a zillion different forms.

Tell me, have you ever experienced moments when someone's cruelty towards you was so intense that it winded you, and stopped you dead in your tracks? You know, those freakish moments when it seemed like a demon had somehow borrowed someone's mouth, and tried to speak death into your spirit? The Bible actually teaches about this dimension of warfare (Luke 22:3, Matthew 16:23).

To illustrate this topic more vividly, I've written a short story called *Melicia Moments*. It will serve as a reference point for the next few chapters, so you'll need to lend me your imagination for a moment.

Melicia Moments

As she shuffles self-consciously towards the living room door, she makes every effort to correct her posture. 'Mustn't hunch your shoulders Melicia,' she tells herself under her breath. Thankfully, a friendly burst of laughter erupts in the corner of the dimly lit room — and she slips in unnoticed. Perfect timing.

The adults have gathered around a mountain of family photos, and are cheerfully discussing old times as Erykah Badu sleepily serenades them from a pair of vintage speakers. Melicia maps out her next few moves. She must bid goodnight to all the guests, and then make a quick beeline for the door before her aunt can spot her.

Meredith, Melicia's aunt, sits furtively studying her niece out of the corner of her eye. Silly cow! The thought floats across her mind like a luminous, red banner. But tonight, she must exercise self-control — she can always indulge herself later. Meredith watches wordlessly as her young niece makes her way around the room. But as Melicia starts to edge her way towards the door, a melancholy expression flickers across Meredith's face. The urge is just too great.

'Where did you get that?' She asks pointing at Melicia's T-shirt.

'A present … from Nan,' replies Melicia wincing, and smiling almost apologetically.

'Hmm very … eye-catching!' says Meredith smiling, but the cobra of hatred has already uncoiled itself in her gut, and her eyelids drip with venom. 'Go and get settled for bed Melicia — I'll be up to see you in a minute.'

Great.

45 minutes elapse before Melicia is tempted to relax a little, but no sooner does she entertain the thought, than she is suddenly aware of her aunt's imposing figure wedged in the doorway of her bedroom.

Melicia knows better than to establish direct eye contact, so she's not quite sure why she doesn't look away. She just stands observing her aunt as if for the first time.

She takes in the beady eyes gleaming with wickedness; the smeared make-up; the bright purple dress straining against the fat belly; the ridiculous wig that has somehow drifted across her head over the course of the evening. Suddenly, she has to bite down on her lower lip to stifle a laugh. Meredith picks up on her niece's uncharacteristic lack of apprehension — and something snaps on the inside of her.

Bounding across the room with the sudden force of a rearing horse, Meredith reaches Melicia in a few quick steps. She grabs her niece's arm, and walks her forcefully over to the full length mirror in the opposite end of the room. The two stand side by side, staring at one another's reflection for a long moment.

Silence.

Meredith is the first to speak.

'Why do you think little girls with pepper grains for hair like to wear pretty lace ribbons Melicia?'

'Not sure Aunty ...' answers Melicia almost inaudibly.

'Hmm. Well, maybe you can tell me this then. Why do little girls with ugly smiles, always try to be the center of attention? I DIDN'T ASK TO BE A PRINCESS, BUT IF THE CROWN FITS!' reads Meredith with an appalled expression.

'A word of advice me darlin' ...' whispers Meredith, engulfing Melicia's nostrils with her sour breath: a lethal cocktail of Bombay mix and hot rum fumes.

Melicia freezes, holding her breath, determined not to let the foul smell enter her body.

'... That T-shirt of yours may fit you honey, but with features like yours, the crown NEVER WILL! Life is very unforgiving of little bitches like you who try to rise above their stations. So do yourself a favour sweetheart — loose the T-shirt! OK princess?' Meredith emphasizes her final word by making quote signs in the air with her fingers. She slips from the room smiling sardonically — her face, the perfect mask of self-satisfaction.

Melicia stands riveted to the spot, studying her own reflection in the mirror. 'With features like mine ...' she whispers to herself.

She'd never noticed before she came to live with Aunt Meredith, how short and fuzzy her hair really was. Or how broadly her nose sat across her dark face, 'Like a bloated black toad preparing to pounce' Meredith would tease.

Her lips too, had become the constant butt of her aunt's jokes, causing a creeping obsession to gradually settle over her. She kept catching herself trying to suck them in whenever she was around people, hoping this would make them appear thinner.

As she stands scrutinizing her features in the mirror, her face suddenly blurs out of focus as two huge tears fill her eyes, and begin to trace the contours of her face. She remains this way for over ten minutes before a single thought suddenly comes floating across her mind, breaking the spell. Soon, there's a whole constellation of thoughts. Thoughts, that start swirling around in her mind like whispers in the wind. The faint whispers belong to the woman whose absence has left a gaping hole in her heart: her grandmother.

She must capture these whispers before it's too late. She must commit them to paper before they become too faint to fathom out any longer.

So, despite the fact that writing is her least favourite thing in the whole world; and despite the fact that her spelling is 'absolutely atrocious!' according to Aunt Meredith, Melicia picks up her half-chewed pencil — and begins to scribble something down on a piece of paper.

Epilouge

Melicia checks her teeth for lipstick, and scrutinizes her appearance in the backlit mirror one last time. She hopes she hasn't overdone it this time. Suit: Armani. Shoes: Jimmy Choo.

She shuts her eyes, and takes a deep breath. 'B-r-e-a-t-h-e!' she tells herself. This case is shaping up to be the biggest of her career so far, the kind that every lawyer secretly dreams of. She must dig deep, pull herself together and bring her A-game on this one. But after doing everything that she can think of to regroup and compose herself, she can't quite figure out why she's still racked with nerves. She has prayed. She has read a couple of scriptures. And yet, she still feels a little … flat. But Melicia has one more 'ace' up her sleeve; something she'd almost forgotten about.

Unzipping one of the compartments of her Fendi hand bag, she carefully pulls out a tattered, well-worn piece of yellow-tinged paper. It's the note that she'd written to herself almost 20 years earlier. It's entitled: NAN'S WORDS.

As she begins to read the note, her eyes begin to twinkle with a radiant — almost mischievous — quality.

NAN'S WORDS

You are buteiful little girl. You are dark skin but the blakker the berry the sweeter the juss. Your lips are not fat ... they are full. One day you will kiss a prince and win his heart. Your feet are big becuz one day you will be tall and eligant. Those feet will carry you to your destinny.

If you ever dout youself remember you are God's favrite child. Melicia darlin you are the fairest of ten thousand. Nanny loves you and Jesus loves you moor.

Returning the note to its place, Melicia slips through the glass doors of the expansive washroom. Walking past marble columns, she makes her way to where a small crowd have gathered. Beneath the high vaulted ceilings of the court house foyer, the members of the press remind her of feral pigeons jostling for bread in the park.

She takes her place beside her client, unfazed by the frenzy of flashing cameras, and the sudden hail of probing questions. Wearing a practiced smile (charming, yet professional) she begins to address the crowd. She begins to talk about the case that has captured the very heart of the nation.

The End

Points To Ponder ...

 ☉ Have you ever had a 'Meredith' in your life? If 'yes' write down the most injurious words, statements or labels that were ever levelled at you.

- ⊘ Melicia survived her circumstances by writing a note to herself. What strategies have you adopted to overcome the effects of negative experiences in your life?

- ⊘ Do you still suffer from the effects of your 'Melicia moments'? What are these effects?

Prayer Time

Dear Lord, thank you for being an invisible cloak of protection around me. I thank you that even when peoples' words, like fiery darts, pierced my confidence and deflated my self-belief, you were there to preserve the essence of who I am. Heavenly father, I am aware that the tongue is tipped with the power of life and death (Proverbs 18:20). So, in your Name, I forgive those who intentionally or unintentionally hurt me with their words. I cancel the effects of every negative comment, and every derogatory label ever planted in my mind. I declare according to your Word in Job 22:28, that:

- ◆ *I am not a victim (1 John 4:4).*

- ◆ *I am a victor (Romans 8:37).*

- ◆ *I am marked for greatness (Jeremiah 1:5).*

- ◆ *I am sentenced to success (Romans 8:29-30) Amen.*

CHAPTER 4

MALICIOUS MOMENTS

If you hear a voice within you say 'you cannot paint,' then by all means paint, and that voice will be silenced.

– Vincent Van Gogh

IF THE EYES are the windows to the soul, then the ears are like little gateways to the future. Whatever you give ear to wields an extraordinary power over you. Whatever you grow accustomed to listening to will mould your ideas, and shape your worldview. This is why you must learn to guard your 'ear gates'. Whoever said 'Sticks and stones may break my bones, but words will never hurt me' must have either been hearing impaired, or else lived a very sheltered life!

The truth is that some of the deepest wounds we carry around with us today, were inflicted on us through that most lethal of all daggers: the tongue. Let's consider what the Bible has to say about this:

> *Death and life are in the power of the tongue ...*
> — Proverbs 18:21 NKJV

> *The hypocrite with his mouth destroys his neighbor ...*
> — Proverbs 11:9 NKJV

In our story, you will have noticed two major influences in Melicia's life: her nan, and her aunt. Two separate individuals diametrically opposed to one another in their motives and in their methods. But were the roles of these two individuals incidental, or was there something more sinister lurking beneath the surface? Were Melicia's nan and aunt just two very different personality types, or had they somehow become two very powerful pieces in a spiritual chess match for her soul?

The Bible teaches us that at any one time in our lives, there are always two forces at work. Two opposing kingdoms furiously battling for 'airtime' in our minds: the Kingdom of God, and the kingdom of darkness. Consider the following scripture:

> *The thief's purpose is to steal and kill and destroy.*
> *My purpose is to give them a rich and satisfying life.*
> — John 10:10 NLT

Like a giant coin spinning furiously above us in the unseen realm, these two domains jostle and fight one another for a place of prominence in our lives: *Heads or Tails.* But unlike in the natural realm, the outcome isn't determined by chance, but by choice.

HEADS

So, the first side of the coin, so to speak, deals with hell's pernicious activities against us: stealing, killing, destroying. Tell me, have you ever felt as though you were born to somehow make a difference in this world?

Perhaps as a child, the conviction was clearer — purer, somehow. But as you grew older and began to be exposed to destiny killers like doubt, disappointment, fear, and heartbreak, you took a wrong turn somewhere in your soul and ended up in a place called *Nowhere!* A wilderness of wickedness where scorpion spirits like scepticism and paranoia skitter around in your mind, robbing you of the notion of who you were meant to be in this world. A place where your dreams, aspirations, and passions are systematically stripped away from you until you hit the dust of desperation, and just begin to expire quietly.

It is often right here in this melancholy labyrinth of aimless wanderings, that many of us die a tiny death. A death imperceptible to most but the reality of which, leaves us hanging from the rafters of yesterdays dreams. Inwardly we 'flat line', but outwardly we cleverly (or not so cleverly) invent sinister little mechanisms to fool everyone around us, that not only are we surviving … we are T-H-R-I-V-I-N-G!

However, once your dream dies, your confidence soon begins to erode. Your vision perishes; and the flame of your faith flounders at the faintest winds of change blowing your way.

All hope for the future evaporates from your heart, and you are left with the sickly residue of what could or should have been (Proverbs 13:12). At this point you have little or no peace at all. And the concept of happiness seems so distant and far-fetched, that even being around joyful people becomes draining.

Those that find themselves suspended in this kind of mental purgatory, are like dead men walking.

Physically they may go on living for the next ten, twenty or even fifty years. But the truth is that they've already been mentally embalmed by a lethal cocktail of lies — mummified until the day of their *actual* funerals.

Some find themselves in this kind of private hell because of an unexpected loss, like the death of a loved one. Others may be trapped there because of the pain of a private betrayal, or the humiliation of a public rejection. But for most of us, it is simply the drip-drip effect of constant disappointments and let-downs that finally cause the collapse of our hope.

Perhaps you find yourself struggling in a similar place right now. But, however broken you may be by recent hardships, I have another one of those announcements for you: **there is another side to this coin!**

TAILS

I call it *tails* because it is revealed at the tail end of John 10:10. It's one of the most vivid pictures of divine intervention that you'll come across in the Bible.

In the latter part of this incredible verse, Jesus interrupts the activities of hell raging against you, and releases a prophetic Word over your life. It's a timeless truth with the power to ignite your spirit and catapult you from where you are to where you belong.

> … *My purpose is to give them a rich and satisfying life.*
> — John 10:10 NLT

Wow! If the Word of God felt like fire in Jeremiah's bones, then this message to you feels like fire in my fingers! Please meditate on the following:

Yes, you've been robbed, stripped and tossed to the side many times. You've been hurt and humiliated more often than you care to remember. You've been used, abused, put down and rejected. And yes, you may feel at times, as though you've been dragged backwards through the hedges of hell. But note one incredible, undeniable, fact:

YOU ARE STILL HERE!

You are still here because the Lord has made it so! He has placed carefully calculated limits to the enemy's power in your life. According to Matthew 16:18, there is a cut-off point to what the enemy is allowed to do to you.

Child of God, your survival has been supernatural. Making it through those unutterable circumstances, prove that you've been pre-selected to be one of life's champions. You are the poster child for Isaiah 54:17, because no weapon maliciously formed against you so far, has been able to prosper. Have you ever wondered why? The Word of God has the answer:

> *When you go through deep waters,*
> *I will be with you.*
>
> *When you go through rivers of difficulty,*
> *you will not drown.*
>
> *When you walk through the fire of oppression, you will*
> *not be burned up; the flames will not consume you.*
>
> — Isaiah 43:2 NLT

When you passed through the darkest ravines of your life, the Lord was there with you. When you were fighting to make it from one sunset to the next, He was right beside you. When all forsook you and left you wasting away in the trenches of yesterday's wars, He was watching over you. Not only did He leave His footprints in the sand, He left tear stains on the ground. For when you cried, He cried. When you ached, He ached. He has always partaken of your pain:

> *This High Priest of ours understands our weaknesses, for he faced all of the same testings we do, yet he did not sin.*
>
> — Hebrews 4:15 NLT

THE SOUND OF YOUR SEASON

Dear friend, perhaps the enemy has been trying to overwhelm you with morbid themes lately. This chapter was written as a siren to your soul. There is a release of a new sound in your life: it's the sound of *breakthrough*. In the spirit realm, the shofar of victory is blowing over you.

The Lord always has the last say in these matters (Psalm 119:89). The verdict is in, and the judgment is final: you are sentenced to success! That rich, abundant life promised at the tail-end of John 10:10, belongs to you.

Believe it. Receive it. Put your best foot forward, and step unto the next rung of the success ladder.

Points To Ponder ...

- Think about some of the most challenging periods of your life. Were there ever times when someone's kindness seemed like a divine intervention?

- During those make-or-break trials, were there ever times when you discovered an inner strength that you never knew you possessed?

- Looking back now, do you feel that surviving and prevailing over such harrowing circumstances, somehow confirms the special calling on your life?

Prayer Time

Dear Lord, thank you for your faithful presence in my life. Thank you for rescuing me repeatedly from the clutches of darkness. Holy Spirit I repent of any wrong decisions or choices that I've made which provided access points for the enemy to attack and torment me.

Through the authority of your Word:

- *I command all doorways open to the enemy in my life, to be immediately shut in the name of Jesus. (Revelation 3:7).*

- *I banish every spirit of discouragement, depression, and disillusionment from my life. (Isaiah 61:3).*

- *I shut down every agent of darkness sent against my life and destiny. (Luke 10:19).*

- *I confess that the shofar of breakthrough is blowing over me. (Psalm 47:5) Amen.*

CHAPTER 5

ONCE UPON A TIME

There is no greater agony than bearing an
untold story inside you.

– Maya Angelou

DEAR FRIEND, WHEN was the last time that you told your story? As a matter of fact, when was the last time that you stopped to consider just how powerful your story really is?

I'd like to remind you that your story is one of the most powerful weapons in your arsenal. It's the one ingredient that makes you stand out from the crowd. Your story is the source of your authority — the x-factor that gives you the right to be heard in this life. In fact, until you find the confidence to start telling your story, your generation will cheerfully ignore and dismiss you. Until your story is told, you will always find yourself fighting for relevance in this world.

Consider this: without his story, Nelson Mandela would have been just another African gentleman in a lovely floral shirt. He would have been just another brother sitting under a Marula tree chatting passionately about the evils of the apartheid system. But his *story*, has etched Mandela's face into our memories forever.

Without her story, Esther might have been just another faceless Jewess swept up in the tides of Old-Testament history.

But at the mere mention of her name, we remember her story and it sets our faith on fire. Her story fills us with the audacity to believe in the promises of God for our own lives.

HISTORY, HER-STORY, YOUR-STORY

Whilst writing *Melicia Moments*, I began to feel like one of those news-hungry reporters in the story. I found myself wishing for a one-hour exclusive with her. I can just picture the interview right now. I wouldn't waste time asking about her recent court case, or her famous client. No. My line of questioning would be much more personal:

- What ever happened to Aunt Meredith?
- How did you overcome such overwhelming odds to become the high-flying lawyer that you are today?
- What's the secret of your confidence?
- Are you dating anyone right now?
- Who does your hair ... is that a weave?

But all joking aside, what makes Melicia's achievements so impressive to us is the little patchwork of information that we have about her story. Likewise, what makes you fascinating to others, doesn't hinge upon the make of your car, the label on the inside of your suit, or the impressive string of fanciful words that you're able to spout every time you open your mouth. No, the thing that will inspire your generation, is the Indiana Jones-type journey that you've had to embark on to become the person that you are today.

That's what we really need to hear: *your story*. So please don't waffle on about your seven-steps-to-your-next-miracle theories, just SHOW ME what God's done for you! Tell me your story.

Consider what the Bible teaches about the power of your story:

> *And they have defeated him by the blood of the Lamb and by their testimony ...*
>
> — Revelation 12:11 NKJV

That's the power of your story (or testimony). Spoken aloud, your story can release a brand new confidence into any atmosphere. Like a flare suddenly fired into a dark night, your story causes hope to rise in the heart of every hearer.

This is what makes your story so powerful. It sends a clear message to the forces of darkness in your region, letting them know that not only do you know who you are — but more importantly — you know *whose* you are!

Your story is like a siren alerting every spirit of wickedness in your path, to retreat back into the shadows because one of the sons/daughters of God has emerged (Romans 8:19). As a case in point, consider the story of one of Israel's greatest kings.

DESTINY'S CHILD

1 Samuel 16 is one of the most powerful portraits of a destiny in the making. After persistently disobeying the Lord, King Saul (the first king of Israel) has just had his kingdom stripped away from him (1 Samuel 15:28). Meanwhile, the Lord instructs Samuel (the prophet) to go to Bethlehem and

anoint one of Jesse's sons as the next king of Israel.

After a nail-biting turn of events, Samuel finally anoints David as the new king of Israel. And with that anointing, we're told that the Spirit of the Lord rested upon him from that day forth. He was never the same again — *but his circumstances certainly were!*

SAME OL' SAME OL'

How strange it must have been for the young David, a humble shepherd boy, to find himself suddenly anointed as the next king of Israel. But stranger still, would have been having to return to business as usual the following day. According to the scriptures, at the time of his dramatic anointing, nothing changed! No throne. No sceptre. No formidable army of warriors to lead. No coverage in Israel's equivalent of *Time* magazine — *nada!*

We're told in the 13th verse that this prophetic event happened in private, within the unremarkable walls of David's family home. It didn't happen in the presence of cheering fans, friends or well wishers. It happened in the midst of those who couldn't quite bring themselves to take him seriously: his family. So, no sooner had his little 'anointing ceremony' reached its conclusion than he was given his marching orders back into the fields of obscurity. But although David returned to his old setting, he did so with a glint in his eye.

Have you ever felt stuck in circumstances that you've simply grown out of? Like trying to party with people you no longer have anything in common with? Or trying to remain romantically involved with someone whom you've quietly moved on from? Or how about working a job that's run its course in your life and leaves you exasperated and drained at the end of each day? Or (here's a good one) how about having to carry out the same set of silly religious 'duties' simply because that's the way it's always been done?

So David returned to his sheep-herding duties. But in the midst of his monotonous routines, the power of his purpose was about to detonate within him, and take him from obscurity to notoriety.

YOU TALKIN' TO ME?

David's debut unfolds like a scene out of Wolfgang Petersen's movie: *Troy*. Close your eyes and picture a circling, shimmering, aerial view of the huge valley of Elah.

Now zoom in, and focus on the colossal form of an Old Testament terrorist named Goliath. At almost ten feet tall, Goliath has almost a whole foot on Robert Pershing Wadlow (the tallest man in medical history).

With a voice that booms out threats from hill to hill across the huge valley, Goliath stands as the ultimate embodiment of opposition to David's future. This guy is talking about overthrowing the kingdom that the Lord has just promised to him (1 Samuel 17:9). So David decides to put the prophesy to the test …

As soon as David hears Goliath's words, observes the reaction of the soldiers, and finds out about the government reward scheme for whoever deals with him, he must have looked up to the heavens and mouthed a silent 'Thank you!'

This was his moment. Goliath's words were no longer addressed to the whole of Israel, they were personal. To David, Goliath wasn't simply a military dilemma to be discussed and debated by the political pundits of his day. No.

Goliath was his opportunity to step into the pages of history.

While others (including Saul) panicked and saw a giant, David looked and saw a giant opportunity! And as we soon discover, his attitude quickly began to determine his altitude.

YOUR HONOUR MAY I TESTIFY

But as David steps forward to take his place in history, he encounters stiff opposition from every angle. David unexpectedly finds himself in a fierce battle even before he descends into the valley to face Goliath. His brothers try to stop him (1 Samuel 17:28), and King Saul begins to interrogate and cross-examine him:

> *"Don't be ridiculous!" Saul replied. "How can a kid like you fight with a man like him? You are only a boy, and he has been in the army since he was a boy!"*
>
> — 1 Samuel 17:33 TLB

It is at this land-mark moment in David's life, that he unleashes the weapon we talked about earlier: his story. What David does next is like a 'Shock And Awe' response against the unseen forces of darkness gathered over his atmosphere. He begins to skilfully tell his story. He carefully begins to catalogue all the victories in his walk with the Lord. It was a watertight strategy that silenced his critics, and left all the agents of hell (Intimidation, Fear, Criticism, Mockery) skittering back into the shadows.

> But David persisted. "When I am taking care of my father's sheep," he said, "and a lion or a bear comes and grabs a lamb from the flock,
>
> I go after it with a club and take the lamb from its mouth. If it turns on me, I catch it by the jaw and club it to death.
>
> I have done this to both lions and bears, and I'll do it to this heathen Philistine too, for he has defied the armies of the living God!
>
> The Lord who saved me from the claws and teeth of the lion and the bear will save me from this Philistine!"
>
> — 1 Samuel 17:34-37a TLB

And what was the result of David's testimony?

> Saul finally consented, "All right, go ahead," he said, "and may the Lord be with you!"
>
> — 1 Samuel 17:37b TLB

The rest is history!

DRESSED FOR SUCCESS

Success came to David that day because he was dressed for it. Although his brothers berated him, the king doubted him, and the king's henchmen probably sniggered at him, he walked confidently into the next chapter of his life using his past successes as stepping stones to the future.

Today, as you boldly step out of the shadows and onto the podium of your purpose, I urge you to remember who you are. Remember whose you are. Never allow yourself to forget how truly inspiring your story is.

Points To Ponder ...

- Where would you say that you invest most of your thoughts: on your successes, or on your slip-ups?
- If you were commissioned by a renowned publisher to tell your story, where would you begin?
- Think of (and if possible write down) some of the most spectacular and unusual facets of your story.

Prayer Time

Dear Lord, thank you for my story. I acknowledge that it is a special and unique gift. I recognise that it's a powerful weapon. I ask you to teach me how to wield it skilfully on the battlefield of everyday life (Psalm 144:1). Holy Spirit I welcome you into my life and ask that you dress me for each battle that I'll face. Please strip me of any ill-fitting spiritual/emotional attire hampering my effectiveness. Through faith in your Word, I now receive:

- *The full armour of God. (Ephesians 6:11).*
- *A victory mindset (Ephesians 6:17).*
- *A breastplate of obedience (Ephesians 6:14).*
- *A belt of heavenly perspectives (Ephesians 6:14).*
- *Boots of redemption (Ephesians 6:15).*

- *A shield of confidence (Ephesians 6:16).*
- *And A sword of revelation knowledge. (Ephesians 6:17) Amen.*

CHAPTER 6

REVELATION REVOLUTIONS

It's not what you look at that matters, it's what you see

– Henry David Thoreau

TELL me, have you ever caught an unexpected glimpse of yourself in a mirror or shop window, and cringed? Have you ever winced at the sound of your own voice on a recording device, or when suddenly presented with unexpected footage of yourself on video?

Do you sometimes find yourself dismissing compliments paid to you, while embracing negative comments like old friends? If you answered 'yes' to any of the above, then perhaps like Melicia, the young girl in our story, you're due for a second opinion. When Melicia stood in front of the mirror after her 'showdown' with Meredith, she found herself at a personal cross roads. She could either continue to view herself through the eyes of a bitter, vindictive woman, or she could choose to start seeing herself through the loving eyes of her late grandmother. Her choice proved to be a pivotal one.

MISSIONARY MUGSHOTS

The way you see yourself can be far more bothersome to you than anything your worst enemy has to throw at you. Your self-image is fundamental to who you become. The opinions that you harbour about yourself, hang like little pictures on the walls of your consciousness, setting the tone and décor for your future.

If you feel that your self-image needs a 'makeover', there's no time like the present. I've met too many individuals so riddled with insecurities that they ended up sabotaging their own chances of success. Some were so afraid of failure that they talked themselves out of launching into the ocean of their dream projects. Instead, they just lingered around at the harbour, remixing and rehashing old excuses.

If this sounds a little too familiar for comfort, then perhaps it's time to start trusting the gifts that the Lord has invested in you:

> *But we have this treasure in earthen vessels, that the*
> *excellence of the power may be of God and not of us.*
> — 2 Corinthians 4:7 NKJV

So then, when you look in the mirror, what do you see? Pause for a moment before giving me your answer. Don't let your response be a reflex action.

To help you along, let's quickly flick through the 'mug shot' album of some of the greatest heroes and she-roes of the Bible. You may be surprised to discover some of the characters that made it onto heaven's Roll of Honour.

The Assassin -

After a spur-of-the-moment homicide on the back streets of Egypt (Exodus 2:12), Moses went on to lead a fledgling nation out of slavery, and into an era of unrivalled miracles.

The Call Girl With A High calling -

After making a name for herself in the Old Testament equivalent of Spearmint Rhino, Rahab emerges from the seedy world of prostitution to take center stage in God's plan. Not only does she save the lives of two Hebrew secret agents (Joshua 2), she goes on to perpetuate the royal line that would eventually give us the Messiah (Matthew 1:5).

The Serial Man Hunter -

After dominating the headlines of every trashy tabloid of her day, the Woman At The Well would seem like the most unlikely candidate to spark a revival. And yet, with a reputation that would make Katie Price blush, she gets converted, receives an anointing to preach the gospel, and successfully evangelizes her entire city (John 4:39).

The Slasher -

After emerging from the ghetto of his day to join Jesus' entourage, Simon 'The Slasher' Peter goes from being handy with a weapon (John 18:10), to being handy with the Word of God. His unique style of preaching triggered a revival that saw thousands come to Christ (Acts 2).

The Hate Preacher -

After graduating from the most prestigious Ivy league collage of his day, the Apostle Paul (formally known as Saul of Tarsus) went on to commit enough acts of terror to warm the heart of every Isis enthusiast (Acts 9:1-2). And yet, his conversion sparked one of the greatest gospel renaissances in history. The list goes on!

CLOSE ENCOUNTERS OF THE GOD KIND

Call me odd, but the thing that blesses me most about our famous five, are their flaws. Their imperfections stand out like huge beacons of promise that there's hope for me yet!

Their faults and blemishes roar like chainsaws, shredding through all my insecurities and fears. Reading about their less-than-perfect lives, I'm suddenly made aware of how much the Lord loves moulding the ordinary into the extraordinary.

But there's something else too, something that links them all together. A common denominator pulsing like a heartbeat beneath the rubble of their addled lives: a good old-fashioned encounter with the living God.

At a time when each of them probably felt like more of a blight on their communities than a blessing; and at a time when they probably found themselves wilting with shame each time they looked in the mirror, the Lord showed up and gave them a virtual tour of their future. I call such moments *Revelation Revolutions!* Have you ever had one of those? Odd, indefinable moments in your life when you kept hearing or seeing the same things over and over again?

Perhaps you had a business idea, or an unusually creative concept. And to your amazement, someone on TV began to talk about a similar product or principle.

Maybe there have been times when you've fallen asleep and had a dream. Nothing unusual there. Except that when you woke up and began your day, unmistakable traces of that same dream began to echo all around you.

Maybe — and this is a particular favourite of mine — you've been contemplating starting a project for a while. But you've been procrastinating and making all kinds of silly excuses. And in the midst of your self-imposed stalemate, you suddenly begin to experience these weird coincidences. Like a personal messaging service, heaven begins to flood you with all these unmistakable confirmations. From billboards in the street, to the random statements of complete strangers, everything just begins to reverberate with the same theme. Like an extra in an episode of *The Twilight Zone*, you suddenly find yourself living in a world where heaven and earth begin to conspire against you, forcing you to get your act together (Jonah 1).

FAITH PHOTOS

There are 'eureka moments' in life that impact us so deeply, that we're never quite the same again. Moments when the Lord opens our eyes and exposes us to the truth of who we really are, and why we were placed on this earth. He grants us a snapshot of the future — a 'faith photo'.

In these mysterious moments, our minds are electrified with sparks from heaven, and our hearts are set ablaze.

Moments like these are so rare, so precious, that they not only inspire us — they define us.

Perhaps for you, such a moment will happen in the middle of a movie, or whilst reading a book. It could happen whilst travelling on a long-distance journey. The Lord is so unpredictable and His visitations so random. Your burning-bush experience could happen anywhere. So keep your eyes peeled and your ears to the ground.

Remember, you have to see it before you can seize it!

Points To Ponder ...

- Create a personalized balance sheet of both your positive and negative traits. You'll probably struggle with the positives. If so, enlist the help of a friend, someone whose opinion you trust. The aim of this exercise is to demonstrate how clearly your gifts outweigh your glitches.

- Write down three Faith Photos (inspired moments) that pinpointed your passions. What were these passions?

- How significantly would your life change if you decided to invest more time, effort and resources on these passions?

Prayer Time

Dear Lord, thank you for making me the person that I am today. I recognise that I've been blessed with unique and uncommon abilities. I repent for not always acknowledging or even recognizing these godly deposits in my life. I thank you for the faithful prompts, reminders and signposts that the Holy Spirit orchestrates in my life. Your Word teaches me that the way I see myself is pivotal to my success (Proverbs 23:7). Therefore, I pray that you would grant me a fresh perspective. By faith, I now declare that:

- *I am not a disappointment to the Lord (Luke 5:8-10).*

- *I am not a disappointment to my family (Luke 20:17).*

- *I am gifted (1 Corinthians 12:7).*

- *I am brimming with divine deposits (2 Corinthians 4:7).*

- *I have a specific assignment, and my gifts were given to me for a unique purpose (Exodus 31:1-5) Amen.*

CHAPTER 7

I HAD A DREAM

The future belongs to those who believe in the beauty of their dreams.

— Eleanor Roosevelt

THE FIRST TIME I met him, he was on the run — and I knew right away that I'd made a friend for life. I hadn't long become a Christian and I desperately needed someone in the bible that I could relate to. Since leaving behind a criminal lifestyle on the backstreets of Birmingham, people like Nehemiah, Daniel and John 'The Beloved', made me nervous. They seemed far too clean-cut for my liking. So, exasperated but undeterred, I continued to plod my way through my Bible readings.

One day, I struck gold! As I picked up my Bible, the pages randomly fell open at the 28th chapter of the book of Genesis. It was a startling discovery: *Dear Brother Jacob* — a man after my own heart. Excited by what I'd found, I quickly flipped back a few chapters and began to read from the 21st verse of Genesis 25. My mouth fell open at what I was reading. As my heart raced, I became transfixed to what I felt was nothing short of a Quentin Tarantino-type storyline.

I began to read about this guy (Jacob) who tricks his brother (Esau) out of his inheritance, steals his 'birthright blessing', and then ends up on the run because his brother puts a contract out on him. *Marvellous!*

(Disclaimer!) In my defence, I *was* only a 'newbie' Christian

To become better acquainted with Jacob's story, please read from Genesis 25, straight through to Genesis 49. But for now, we'll take up the story from the last few verses of Genesis 27.

TOO KINETIC TO CONNECT

So Esau hated Jacob because of what he had done to him. He said to himself, "My father will soon be gone, and then I will kill Jacob."

But someone got wind of what he was planning and reported it to Rebecca. She sent for Jacob and told him that his life was being threatened by Esau.

"This is what to do," she said. "Flee to your Uncle Laban in Haran.

Stay there with him awhile until your brother's fury is spent, and he forgets what you have done.

Then I will send for you. For why should I be bereaved of both of you in one day?"

— Genesis 27:41-45 TLB

The moment Jacob hears about his brother's homicidal tendencies towards him — understandably — he panics and goes on the run.

Fear often does this to us. It's the spectre that sends us scarpering off in the opposite direction of our calling. Fear addles the mind and turns us into frightened fugitives. It leaves us blindly trying to outrun imaginary phantoms.

In my mind's eye I see a disorientated Jacob, lumbering forward and stumbling over loose rocks. I see him desperately trying to put as much distance between himself and his troubled past. But things could have been so different.

Had he paused to hear from heaven on his way to Haran, he might have caught a glimpse of one of the most dynamic lives in the Old Testament: *his own!*

Remember that well-worn statement echoing down through the ages that everyone utters at one point or the other in their lifetime?

IF I ONLY KNEW THEN WHAT I KNOW NOW ...

Imagine how differently Jacob might have interpreted this period of his life, had he known that it was written in his destiny to:

- Become the next great Patriarch of the Jewish people.

- Marry four wives who would battle for his affection, and grapple with each other for the opportunity to bare him children.

- Watch angels ascend and descend from heaven, and actually wrestle a blessing out of one of them.

- Produce a daughter, numerous grandchildren, and twelve sons who would go on to have the tribes of a new nation named after them.

- Spend his retirement years in a palace because one of his sons would rise to prominence in one of the most powerful nations of his day.

I wonder how differently a glimpse of his future, might have affected his choices?

But as long as Jacob remained panic-stricken and paranoid, his vision remained scrambled. As long as he was preoccupied with worrying about whether the present day would be his last, he was unable to perceive let alone believe in God's plan for his life (2 Corinthians 2:14). In his frantic state, he was simply too kinetic to connect with heaven's agenda.

Now, when the Lord is unable to get through to Jacob, He waits for him to fall asleep — and then He ambushes him with precious promises. Let's read what happens to our motionless runaway.

> At sundown he arrived at a good place to set up camp and stopped there for the night. Jacob found a stone to rest his head against and lay down to sleep.
>
> As he slept, he dreamed of a stairway that reached from the earth up to heaven. And he saw the angels of God going up and down the stairway.
>
> At the top of the stairway stood the Lord, and he said, "I am the Lord, the God of your grandfather Abraham, and the God of your father, Isaac. The ground you are lying on belongs to you. I am giving it to you and your descendants.
>
> Your descendants will be as numerous as the dust of the earth! They will spread out in all directions—to the west and the east, to the north and the south. And all the families of the earth will be blessed through you and your descendants.
>
> What's more, I am with you, and I will protect you wherever you go. One day I will bring you back to this land. I will not leave you until I have finished giving you everything I have promised you."

Then Jacob awoke from his sleep and said, "Surely the Lord is in this place, and I wasn't even aware of it!"

But he was also afraid and said, "What an awesome place this is! It is none other than the house of God, the very gateway to heaven!"

— Genesis 28:11-17 NLT

THE DREAM GATE

Reading this story, I was suddenly ushered into another one of those 'revelation revolutions'. When we can no longer hear God's voice over the 'noise' of our circumstances, the Lord will often make a stealthy approach through what I like to call: *The Dream Gate.*

Consider the following scriptures:

*For God speaks again and again,
though people do not recognize it.*

*He speaks in dreams, in visions of the night,
when deep sleep falls on people
as they lie in their beds.*

*He whispers in their ears
and terrifies them with warnings.*

*He makes them turn from doing wrong;
he keeps them from pride.*

*He protects them from the grave,
from crossing over the river of death.*

— Job 33:14-18 NLT

During the Easter of 1998, I had a faith crisis.

I'd been single for over seven years since becoming a Christian, and the strain of being on my own for so long had caught me completely off guard.

Now at the time, there were a number of quite promising prospects in our local church, and I felt quite positive about finding my future wife. The problem, was that there were those in my new 'church family' that felt that my dramatic conversion to Christianity, was just a little too good to be true. Consequently, I found myself being quietly ostracised by the 'blue bloods' of the church.

I noticed that whenever I developed an interest in a young lady and began to make any kind of attempt to speak to her, she would be 'fenced off' by family members, or some plain-clothes elder on 'patrol duties'. This happened so many times that after a while, I began to feel like an outcast. I started to wonder whether I had the words: WATCH OUT LEPER ABOUT, stencilled on my face.

I can smile about it now, but at the time I felt crushed. It was like being trapped in a personal siege. The constant rejection gradually wore me down, causing me to question God's providence in my life.

WOMAN OF MY DREAMS

One night when I could no longer bear the burden of my situation, it all seemed to come crashing down around me. I broke down on my bedroom floor and just wept. There were no words. No prayers. There were neither petitions, nor protests — I simply cried myself into a deep, restless sleep.

Suddenly, I found myself transported into a dream that gives me goose bumps to this day.

I dreamt that I was briskly walking through a huge field. As I walked, I became aware that I was supposed to be meeting a group of people at the top of the field. But when I arrived at the designated spot, they were nowhere to be seen. The disappointment I felt, was *palpable*.

As I stood disorientated and completely at a loss as to what to do next, I saw a young lady approaching me in the distance. As she drew nearer, I noticed that she wore a similar expression on her face to the one I had on mine. She introduced herself to me and began to explain that she'd been hoping to meet with a group of people at this spot. But now, she feared that she'd been 'stood up'.

I remember looking deep into her eyes for a long moment before speaking my mind.

'Well,' I began, 'if the people we were supposed to meet let us down, why don't we travel together?'

Her face suddenly opened up in a shy, tentative smile, and she nodded her consent. As I extended my hand towards her, she reached for it, holding onto me with a trust that warmed my dreaming heart. But the 'cherry on the cake' was what happened next. The moment we joined hands, the scenery was immediately transformed before us. From a sleepy sepia-toned atmosphere, the scene suddenly burst into sparks of new life. There was an implosion of living colour.

As we walked hand in hand, we found ourselves in the middle of an Eden-esque garden. A place striking, and resplendent with the sounds and smells of spring in full bloom.

In my dream, I remember thinking about the symbolism of it all. It seemed to be a resounding confirmation of the one thing that I desperately needed to know:

MY EVE WAS ON HER WAY.

Hallelujah!

When I awoke from my dream, I felt as though my heart had been healed (Psalm 107:20). I returned to everyday life with a knowing little smile on the inside of me. All insecurities about finding my wife had been completely erased from my thoughts — *I had heard from heaven.*

Two weeks later, the young lady that I had dreamt about (who was also a new Christian in our church) approached me, asking if we could talk. It seemed quite urgent so I obliged. I remember her looking nervous and agitated — to say the least. She began the conversation something like this:

'Ok. So I have something to share with you that's going to sound crazy!'

'Try me,' I said.

'Well,' she continued, flushing with embarrassment, 'I think the Lord is telling me that you're … my … my … h-u-s-b-a-n-d.' This last bit came out almost as a whisper.

'I told you it would sound crazy!' she said breaking eye contact.

'I wasn't going to say anything' she continued, 'but it's just that the other night I had this weird dream about you … I mean, *us*.' Encouraged by the intrigued expression on my face, she steeled herself and soldiered on.

'You see, I was in this field to meet some folks but they

stood me up! You were there, and I think you'd been jilted too. So you came up with this crazy plan about us going together. But what really blew me away, was what happened the moment our hands connected! Everything became *sooooo* green! There were rivers ... and waterfalls ... and ...'

She stopped mid-sentence because I had taken over. I began to describe (in great detail) the scenery of her (our) dream. The young lady sat stunned at what she was hearing. Then there was this eerie silence between us. We just sat staring at one another in utter shock: *we had already spoken to one another in the realm of our dreams!*

A month later, I produced a ring and proposed to her. She asked me what had taken me so long — and accepted! Exactly one year to the date, we were joined together as man and wife.

It's been almost sixteen years since then, and we're still in love. We're still unfolding the mysteries of our Eden together.

LIVING THE DREAM

As we bring this chapter to a close, I cannot overstate the importance of paying close attention to your dreams. Learning to recall, interpret, and live out your God-given dreams, will give you the edge in life. Now for five fascinating facts about dreams.

The Lord sometimes uses dreams to:

1. Warn us of impending danger.
Now when they had departed, behold, an angel of the Lord Child and His mother, flee to Egypt, and stay there until I

bring you word; for Herod will seek the young Child to destroy Him." (Matthew 2:13 NKJV).

2.Give us specific instructions.

Then in my dream, the angel of God said to me, 'Jacob!' And I replied, 'Yes, here I am.' "The angel said, 'Look up, and you will see that only the streaked, speckled, and spotted males are mating with the females of your flock. For I have seen how Laban has treated you. I am the God who appeared to you at Bethel, the place where you anointed the pillar of stone and made your vow to me. Now get ready and leave this country and return to the land of your birth." (Genesis 31:11-13 NLT).

3.Identify our life partner.

But while he thought about these things, behold, an angel of the Lord appeared to him in a dream, saying, "Joseph, son of David, do not be afraid to take to you Mary your wife, for that which is conceived in her is of the Holy Spirit. (Matthew 1:20 NKJV).

4. Give us a glimpse of the future.

As he slept, he dreamed of a stairway that reached from the earth up to heaven. And he saw the angels of God going up and down the stairway. At the top of the stairway stood the Lord, and he said, "I am the Lord, the God of your grandfather Abraham, and the God of your father, Isaac. The ground you are lying on belongs to you. I am giving it to you and your descendants." (Genesis 28:12-14 NLT).

5. Warn off our enemies.

Just then, as Pilate was sitting on the judgment seat, his wife sent him this message: "Leave that innocent man alone. I suffered through a terrible nightmare about him last night." (Matthew 27:19 NLT).

Points To Ponder ...

- Think about (and if possible, write down) three dreams that you've had that you believe were God-given. What was it about these dreams that made them stand out from the rest? What was their relevance (if any) to your past, present or future?

- Consider carefully what might have happened had Pharaoh (Genesis 41), or Joseph (Matthew 1: 20), ignored their dreams. Could it be possible that the solution to some of your dilemmas have already been revealed through the realm of your dreams realm?

- Do you prepare yourself for revelatory dreams, paying careful attention to the things that you watch, listen to, or focus on before going to sleep at nights?

Prayer Time

Dear Lord, thank you for the mystery of dreams. I now recognise that my dreams often serve as avenues of instruction, direction, warning and preparation. I pray for the gift of interpretation: please help me make sense of what I dream. I also thank you for my daytime dreams: the ones that you planted in my heart since childhood. I pray for the skills, strategies and strength of character to live out those dreams. With the help of the Holy Spirit, I now declare that through my dreams:

- *I will receive Power-Point presentations of the future (Genesis 37:5-11).*

- *I will be alerted of danger (Matthew 2:13).*

- *I will receive divine strategies (Genesis 31:11-13).*

- *I will receive divine 'intel' about individuals that belong in my life (Matthew 1:20).*

- *I will receive divine 'intel' about individuals that do not belong in my life (Genesis 20:3-10) Amen.*

PART II
THE AMBUSH

DESTROYING THE

SEVEN DESTINY

KILLERS

And from the days of John the Baptist until now the kingdom of heaven suffers violence, and the violent take it by force

Matthew 11:12 NKJV

CHAPTER 8

FEAR

Faith activates God - Fear activates the Enemy.

– Joel Osteen

I WOULD LIKE to begin this new section with a quick confession. I've spent half of my life in a hostage crisis! Incarcerated, not by Al-Qaeda or Isis or any other crazed terror group, but by a single spirit. A spirit so relentless, so cunning, that it managed to morph itself into one of the most formidable of all the destiny killers out there: FEAR.

I discovered (the hard way) that until I was prepared to engage in an all-out war with this spirit, I would never be free. I would never quite master the subtle art of being me.

And so, like any good war strategist, I decided to carry out some research on my enemy. I wanted to build up an in-depth profile of him: something that I could pin up onto the wall of my consciousness. I needed something to serve as a constant reminder never to entertain this awful spectre.

THE GENESIS OF FEAR

The first time we meet him in the Bible, he is undercover. He is almost undetectable. There is no mention of him directly. In fact, had it not been for the melancholy ramblings of Adam after the fall, we may never have detected Fear's presence in the garden of Eden at all.

Observe closely:

> He replied, *"I heard you walking in the garden, so I hid.*
> ***I was afraid*** *because I was naked."*
>
> — Genesis 3:10 (Emphasis mine) NLT

There! Did you spot it? Adam the crown of God's creation; Adam the majestic being who traversed Eden's expanse as heaven's regent on earth; Adam the Patriarch-prince who gave definition to every other creature on earth, was suddenly cowering in the corner trying to fight off a panic attack! For the very first time in his life, he was **afraid**! It seems that once Adam and Eve sinned, the door was suddenly flung open to a number of other assailants.

Satan had a plan. He needed to ensnare the first couple in a web of deceit. He then needed to attack their relationship with God. He managed the first phase single-handedly, but in order to pull off the second, he needed help.

It was then that an unholy alliance was formed. A lifelong partnership in hell that still has most of humanity reeling to this day. As Satan handed the baton over to his new partner, Fear simply stepped forward and did his thing. He released black clouds of anxiety, panic and worry into Eden's atmosphere. Consequently, a sickening reflex action was birthed in mankind: the urge to run from God.

Instead of running *to* God the Father (the source of rescue) Adam and Eve found themselves running *from* God. Unfortunately, humanity is still on the run to this day!

❦

FACING THE PHANTOM OF FEAR

I was a child when I first met Him. His first appearance in my life was in the corner of my bedroom: an ominous, floating figure (which actually turned out to be my school coat).

At times, Fear would shape-shift into a nameless presence under my bed. He was a slippery fellow too. He always managed to evaporate into thin air whenever I risked a manic peek behind doors, or inside half-open wardrobes.

But I grew up.

And when I was no longer afraid of the dark, and when I had become immune to Fear's more overt shenanigans, he went under cover.

He launched himself into a cunning kind of guerrilla warfare. He would camouflage himself in the dense jungle of my circumstances, and carry out terror attacks at the worst possible moments. He'd wait for the defining moments in my life. Moments that weren't likely to come back around again in a hurry. Then he would sidle up to me and calmly whisper worse-case-scenarios into my spirit. Using hell's best technology, he would beam 3D images of abject failure onto the screen of my mind.

Fear proved to be a formidable foe, and before long, I feared everything.

- I feared failure: not becoming all that friends, family and foes expected me to be.

- I feared poverty: not being able to make ends meet and provide for my family.

- I feared ill health: every symptom became a screaming

siren of something terminal.

- I feared loosing loved ones: I lived on tenterhooks, wondering whether the next call would be 'the dreaded one'.

- I feared not fitting in with the crowd: so I invented numerous personas — which I then feared would be unmasked at any moment.

- I feared rejection: not being accepted by others.

- I even feared success: in case it didn't last!

- But above all, I feared death. I suffered from Hammer-house-of-horror type nightmares about waking up dead! I would imagine myself dying and having some kind of permanent out-of-body experience. I'd look on helplessly as the ear-splitting screams of my loved ones ripped through the air. *'But…I'm right here!'* I would desperately cry, in a faint, fading voice.

FEARLESS

I prayed to the Lord, and he answered me.
He freed me from all my fears.

— Psalms 34:4 NLT

The spirit of Fear is the worst taskmaster that you can ever live under. His work of bondage knows no bounds. Fear has so many tentacles that his presence in your life will make you feel as though you're facing a legion of attackers. Using everything from seemingly harmless phobias to full-blown meltdowns, Fear will cripple your confidence. He'll turn you into a parody of the creative, wholesome person that the Lord intended you to be.

In the summer of 2008, I was in Africa on a preaching assignment when my rescue from Fear finally came. I remember at the time, I had been reading *Welcome Holy Spirit* by Benny Hinn (Thomas Nelson, Inc.).

In his book, Hinn recounts some of the encounters that he'd had with the Holy Spirit. Hinn describes how tangible the presence of the Lord would be during such visitations. So much so, that he'd often find it difficult to remain standing. He spoke about the Holy Spirit as though He was an *actual* person. I sat stunned by what I had read. Imagine experiencing God on such a level. *You'd fear absolutely nothing and no one after such an encounter,* I reasoned.

Now, I wish I could tell you that I offered up a serene, saint-like prayer to the Lord at this point. Truth be told, I flipped out! I frisbeed the book across the room (sorry Pastor Benny) and unleashed a verbal tirade into the air.

'Lord,' I began, 'why have you left me in this sorry state for so long? And how is it that you've been so quick to "appear" to your other servants like Benny Hinn?'

'Am I the monkey's uncle, or something?' I ranted. 'Well, to be honest Jesus … I'm not impressed!!!!'

Now, don't you just love the Lord's patience? Had we been in Old Testament times, I shudder to think what might have happened to me for such insolence. But the Lord must have looked past my uncouth prayer because that night while I was asleep, something happened …

At around 3 am that morning, my bedroom door opened … and shut again. I heard the Lord's footsteps walking towards my bed. How did I know it was the Lord? Every inch of my body just *knew*. No phrase in the Oxford dictionary could describe how I felt. Every fibre of my being just wanted to hit the deck, and start worshipping!

But I couldn't.

I was somehow suspended in that hard-to-define place: somewhere between wakefulness and sleep. A place where although you're aware of your surroundings, you've not quite woken up yet. The Lord's footsteps paused right by my bedside. Then, He extended His finger and — the only way that I can describe it — poked my soul!

At that instant, I shot bolt upright in bed, my mind spinning cartwheels. Oddly, at that instant, I was also aware of another presence in the corner of the room: Fear.

I heard the Lord walk around to the other side of my bed (remember I was fully awake at this point). A part of me (albeit a very small part) wanted to turn around and see the owner of the footsteps. But I knew that my heart would never have been able to endure anything more intense than audible footsteps. I had challenged the Lord to show up … and (God help me) here He was.

I must confess, I was terrified. You see, as I mentioned before, the spirit of Fear was also present. I could sense him cowering in the corner of my room. I caught my breath and finally managed to address the Lord. I said something like: 'OK Jesus, I know I asked you to be more tangible to me … but surely you can't expect me to be OK with all of this!'

Isn't it amazing how we always want the penny *and* the bun? My prayer-tantrum had ushered me into one of the greatest God-encounters that I'd ever experienced, and here

I was whining about how scary it was: typical! But The Lord is a tender-hearted Father. What He did next, changed my life forever. He spoke to me. It wasn't a lengthy prophetic message. Neither was it an earth-shattering speech. It was just a simple instruction. He said: '**FEAR NOT!**'

At the sound of this audible command, my world changed in a moment. It felt as though Fear just withered and died in the corner of that room. Something like a nuclear detonation went off in the 'spirit realm', and a billowing cloud of God's glory came rolling over the landscape of my life.

This glory cloud seemed poisonous to every manifestation of Fear in my life. All manifestations of fear in my life from the smallest, to the most heavy-duty ones (like the fear of death), were suddenly gone. It was one of the most incredible moments in my walk with the Lord.

Like any normal person I have things that still make me uncomfortable, but those deep-rooted fears that used to rob me of my peace and strip me of my sense of joy, have been permanently put out of action!

❧

Are you living life to the full right now, or is Fear sabotaging your walk at every turn? What great accomplishments are being held back in your life because of your fears? Consider for a moment what might have happened (or not happened) had Martin Luther not had the courage to hammer his 95 theses on the door of the Castle church at Wittenberg? Or, imagine what a huge loss to the Civil Rights movement it might have been, had Rosa Parks 'caved in' at the moment of truth, and just shuffled off to the back of the bus to quietly settle down with the 60s version of a lottery scratch-card. But, most sobering of all, try and picture for a moment where you and I would have been had Jesus not found the courage to say:

> *"Now My soul is troubled, and what shall I say?*
> *'Father, save Me from this hour'? But for this purpose*
> *I came to this hour.*
>
> — John 12:27 NKJV

Dear friend, you have been blessed with a remarkable destiny, one that will require every ounce of courage, and temerity that you have. There is no room for Fear in your life. This is a God-appointed hour, please do not allow the spirit of Fear to loiter within the gates of your assignment.

Now for 5 powerful facts about Fear:

1. Fear will distance you from the Lord.
So he said, "I heard Your voice in the garden, and I was afraid because I was naked; and I hid myself." (Genesis 3:10 NKJV).

2. Fear will empower the enemy to attack you.
For the thing I greatly feared has come upon me,
And what I dreaded has happened to me (Job 3:25 NKJV).

3. Fear will hinder you from walking in the miraculous.
So He said, "Come." And when Peter had come down out of the boat, he walked on the water to go to Jesus. But when he saw that the wind was boisterous, he was afraid; and beginning to sink he cried out, saying, "Lord, save me!" (Matthew 14:29-30 NKJV).

4. Fear closes the door on the promises of God for your life.

... they certainly shall not see the land of which I swore to their fathers, nor shall any of those who rejected Me see it. But My servant Caleb, because he has a different spirit in him and has followed Me fully, I will bring into the land where he went, and his descendants shall inherit it. (Numbers 14:23-24 NKJV).

5. Fear is not just a feeling, it is a wicked spirit with a malicious agenda.

For God has not given us a spirit of fear, but of power and of love and of a sound mind. (2 Timothy 1:7 NKJV).

Points To Ponder ...

- Write down five of your most disturbing fears. Are you able to identify the root of these fears. When, where, and how did these fears first begin to manifest in your life?

- Can you identify the triggers for these anxieties? When are you most vulnerable to them?

- Have you ever allowed yourself to become obsessively fearful about a situation, only to experience a spectacular turnaround in the end? Consider how different your life might be if you no longer lived in the grip of Fear. Would you dream bigger, reach higher, love more deeply?

Prayer Time

Dear Lord, I recognise that Fear did not come from you. I refuse to remain under its rule (2 Timothy 1:7). I acknowledge that Fear has been a gateway, and an access point for the enemy to operate in my life (Job 3:25). Therefore, in the Mighty Name of Jesus, I slam shut every doorway, gateway, window, trapdoor and any other point of access that I have knowingly/unknowingly opened up to the enemy through my fears. Through faith in your Word, I now declare that:

- *I am released from all my fears (Psalms 34:4).*

- *I possess all the necessary components to stand my ground against the enemy (1 John 4:4).*

- *I have inherited a new posture of boldness in my mind, heart, speech and body language (Proverbs 28:1).*

- *I am free from the devices of the enemy designed to instil fear and intimidation into my psyche (Isaiah 54:17) Amen.*

CHAPTER 9

DOUBT

Our doubts are traitors, and make us lose the good we oft might
win, by fearing to attempt.

– William Shakespeare

I F FEAR WAS a farmer, then *doubt* would be his most
precious seed. A compulsive sower, Fear will roam through
an individual's life planting neat rows of cynicism, suspicion,
scepticism and mistrust wherever possible. Seeking out the
soft soil of an unsuspecting mind, Fear will carefully sprinkle
seeds of doubt, knowing that they will later spring up as
thorns. These thorns then begin to choke out every seedling
of creativity and self-belief that we possess. Maybe you've
been there before?

You know how gifted you are, and what you're capable of
once you put your mind to it. But therein lies the problem:
putting your mind to it! Each time you try mentally putting
your best foot forward, you become riddled with doubts.
You just freeze. And the most frustrating thing about this
dimension of warfare, is that you can be in the right place
at the right time, and still not take that all-important step
forward. Sound familiar?

THORNY THOUGHTS

And some fell among thorns, and the thorns sprang up with it and choked it.

— Luke 8:7 NKJV

I can think of no greater depiction of a thorn, than one of those nasty little thoughts that pops into your head and crushes your confidence in a moment. As a case in point, lets consider the story of a young man (whom I'll call Thomas for now) who approached me for pastoral counselling one Sunday afternoon.

The young man seemed nervous and preoccupied. He had only recently wedded. In fact, this had been the couple's first Sunday back in church since their wedding. After a noisy and animated welcome back into the church family, I noticed that Thomas seemed somewhat unsettled in himself. He seemed to be silently trying to communicate something to me.

After the service, he finally approached me. But before I could complete my greeting, I was interrupted by a desperate plea: 'Pastor please help me!' After making some arrangements — which had to be handled delicately as I was only a visiting speaker at Thomas's local church — we finally met up for a chat.

Thomas began to recount how excited he and his new bride had been on their wedding night. After a seemingly endless battle with lust, the newly-weds were beside themselves with excitement as they bid goodnight to their guests, and beat a hasty retreat to their honeymoon suit. As his wife shyly retreated to the luxury of their en suite bathroom to prepare for their big night, Thomas could barely contain his excitement. But, as Thomas lay waiting for his beautiful bride to emerge, Fear quietly floated by, dispatching a single seed into the soft soil of his unguarded mind. It was a seed of doubt. A devilish little kernel that reached its target with relative ease. Germinating instantly, the seed took root and sprang up into a tree. A talking tree. It simply said: 'CONGRATULATIONS!'

Continuing, it said, 'SUCH A GRAND AND SPLENDID WEDDING ... TAKES A REAL MAN TO PULL OFF SOMETHING SO ... DAZZLING. LET'S JUST HOPE THAT YOU'LL BE ABLE TO PERFORM WELL AT THE FINALE"! YOU KNOW ... WITH IT BEING SUCH A LONG DAY ... LET'S JUST HOPE IT WON'T BE A PITIFULLY SHORT NIGHT!

It was a simple line of attack, but the delivery was exact. Thomas began to fidget, instantly becoming agitated at the intrusive thought. Wiping a thin film of sweat from his forehead, he suddenly realised that instead of eagerly anticipating the appearance of his beautiful bride from the bathroom, he was now dreading the sound of the door opening. So, he just lay motinless on the bed — waiting for the inevitable ...

When the door finally opened, Thomas *knew* he was in trouble. He described what felt like a cold shower washing over him, leaving him privately fighting off a panic attack. In what seemed like the unfolding of a slow-motion scene, Thomas watched his bride approaching him with all the promise of a rare flower in full bloom. And as his young wife proceeded to offer herself to him with utter abandon, Thomas recalled how to his horror, he began to feel himself shrinking inwardly — and outwardly!

'Are you ok sweetie?' His wife gently inquired.

'Err … yes … I … I think I must just be exhausted. I'm so sorry'.

As his wife lovingly stroked his head, whispering gentle words of affirmation into his ear, Thomas slowly turned his back to her. He just lay motionless, silently staring at the stunning painting on the wall. It was a modern piece depicting a couple intertwined in a sensual embrace. But as Thomas continued to study the picture, it suddenly morphed out of shape as huge tears pooled in his eyes, and began to run down his face and unto his pillow.

The tears were still flowing in my office as Thomas concluded his version of events. He began to confess to feelings of self-loathing and shame. It had been almost two weeks since their wedding and their marriage still hadn't been consummated yet.

When I began to speak, my words were not addressed to Thomas — but to an old, familiar spirit: Fear (the doubt sower). As I started to pray, I stood in the Name of the Lord Jesus Christ and began to assert divine authority over the presence, plans and produce of that spirit. The atmosphere immediately shifted! I continued to voice aggressive decrees, quoting the following scripture:

> *A fire goes before Him, And burns up His enemies round about.*
>
> — Psalms 97:3 NKJV

I began to release the fire of God against every seed of doubt, and against every evil root working against the precious couple.

As I prayed, I sensed a change in Thomas too. His eyes widened at the implications of my prayers. Suddenly realising that he'd been under some kind of spiritual attack, a bright light seemed to switch on somewhere in his mind. Rising to his feet, he began to pace the floor of my office, praying more aggressively and determinedly than I'd ever seen or heard him pray before: *a man at war!* Satisfied that he'd assassinated every enemy on the horizon, he suddenly declared: 'Heavenly Father, by faith, I receive the anointing of Joshua to **ENTER THE PROMISE LAND!'**

With that, he thanked me and left, with the kind of expression that William 'Brave heart' Wallace would have been proud of!

According to Thomas' pastor, when he walked into church the following Sunday, he did so with the look of a man who had just won the Nobel Peace Prize for his part in the abolition of slavery: *his own!* Thomas was a free man. He had routed every enemy undermining his marriage, and had entered his promise land with ease and with the Lord's blessing.

DOUBTING THOMAS

Are you in danger of missing out on your miracle because of your miserable doubts? Perhaps like Thomas you find your destiny being hijacked by unwanted thoughts. It's vital to recognise that doubts are demonic darts tipped with poison, to paralyse every joyful moment in your life.

As Thomas discovered and dismantled the real source of his setbacks, so must you. I encourage you to identify, and free yourself from every thought injuring your mind.

Like Thomas, make a decision to *war* rather than *worry*; to *fight* rather than *faint*; to *subdue* rather than *surrender*. Make a decision today never to allow doubts to poison your atmosphere. You are blessed, and there's no *doubt* about that!

The following are 5 things you should know about doubt.

1.The Bible refers to doubt as evil.

Beware, brethren, lest there be in any of you an evil heart of unbelief in departing from the living God; (Hebrews 3:12 NKJV).

2.Doubt corrupts faith.

Afterward the disciples asked Jesus privately, "Why couldn't we cast out that demon?" "You don't have enough faith," Jesus told them. "I tell you the truth, if you had faith even as small as a mustard seed, you could say to this mountain, 'Move from here to there,' and it would move. Nothing would be impossible. (Matthew 17:19-20 NLT).

3.Doubt blocks God's intervention in your life.

Now He did not do many mighty works there because of their unbelief (Matthew 13:58 NKJV).

4.Doubt prevents the fulfilment of your God-given dreams.

So we see that they could not enter in because of unbelief. (Hebrews 3:19 NKJV).

5. Doubt makes your character unstable.

But let him ask in faith, with no doubting, for he who doubts is like a wave of the sea driven and tossed by the wind. For let not that man suppose that he will receive anything from the Lord; he is a double-minded man, unstable in all his ways (James 1:6-8 NKJV).

Points To Ponder ...

- Write a list of the most destructive doubts that often run through your mind.

- How are these doubts imported into your mind? Does the enemy use particular individuals or circumstances to sow these seeds of uncertainty into your thinking?

- How do you typically respond to these doubts? How different would your world-view be if you were free from such damaging thoughts?

Prayer Time

Dear Lord, thank you for being my provider. In you I have everything that I need (2 Peter 1:3). Through you, I can do all things (Philippians 4:13). You will never lead me into a challenge that I can't handle (1 Corinthians 10:13). Heavenly Father I bring every seed of doubt that has ever been sown into my mind before you now. In accordance with Matthew 13:30, I now receive your refining fire. Holy Spirit, reduce to ashes, every thought, notion, opinion or attitude that is contrary to your plan for my life.

I now declare that through you:

- *I am able to do whatever I put my mind to (Mark 9:23).*

- *I am able to fulfil my God-given purpose on earth (Philippians 1:6).*

- *I possess an armoury of unique gifts (2 Corinthians 4:7).*

- *I am an original (Psalm 139:14).*

- *I am successful (Deuteronomy 28:1-14) Amen.*

CHAPTER 10

PROCRASTINATION

Procrastination is the bad habit of putting off until the day after tomorrow what should have been done the day before yesterday.

– Napoleon Hill

TELL ME DEAR friend, what are you waiting for?

You are blessed. You are beautiful. And you are already beginning to blossom into that rare wonder that God designed you to be. So what's wrong? What's stopping you from stepping into your purpose: that stunning future prepared for you at some untraceable point in eternity past?

Maybe there are lots of reasons why you haven't stepped out yet. But what if those reasons were nothing more than cleverly disguised red herrings? Devilish diversions designed to trick you into squandering the most valuable asset that you have: *time*.

If there's one thing I've learnt in over twenty years of ministry and counselling, it's this: life's victims aren't so much those who run out of money, friends or sponsors. No. Life's true casualties are those who run out of time. As I've sat praying with precious souls on their deathbeds over the years, I've looked into too many eyes and seen that most dreaded of all emotions: regret.

- Dreams that were never actualised.
- Broken relationships left unmended.

- Gifts, talents, and unique abilities left to waste.
- Lost opportunities for a rich relationship with God.

I noticed that whenever the subject came up (as it inevitably did) as to what — if given the opportunity — could have been done differently, the answers almost always came back the same:

'I would have spent more time with my children/family.'

'I would have invested more time in my personal dreams.'

'I would have been a better steward of my time.'

The list goes on.

Now, It's difficult to keep hearing such heart-felt cries over and over again without being struck by one irrefutable truth: time is priceless.

TIME ISN'T MONEY

Every commodity on earth from crude oil to gold bullion, once lost, can be recovered. But what separates time from every other resource on earth, is that once spent, it can never be recaptured. I also discovered that the pound sterling isn't the most powerful currency in the world. Neither is the dollar or the yen. These currencies fluctuate in value every day.

The value of the time-currency however, is immeasurable. The more time you spend on this earth, the less you will have of it — and therefore the more valuable it will become to you. To accomplish your goals and see your dreams materialise, you must learn to harness this most valuable of all resources. To succeed, one must learn to budget time skilfully.

To emphasise the importance of good time management, I've compiled a loose handful of some of my favourite 'time' quotes:

Whatever you want to do, do it now! There are only so many tomorrows.

— Pope Paul VI

Better three hours too soon, than one minute too late.

— William Shakespeare

Don't count every hour in the day, make every hour in the day count.

— Unknown

All that really belongs to us is time; even he who has nothing else has that.

— Baltasar Gracian

Time is the wisest counsellor of all.

— Pericles

I must work the works of Him who sent Me while it is day; the night is coming when no one can work.

— Jesus Christ

Now that we've talked about the 'time thing', I'd like to pose a question to you. If you suddenly discovered that today was to be your final day on earth, how would you feel? Would you sit back and smile at your accomplishments, or would you feel slightly alarmed at your 'mission unaccomplished'? Would you be able to look back with contentment at a life well lived? Or would you feel slightly sickened at the thought of a bunch of unfulfilled plans, and a catalogue of unused gifts?

Ah, yes, but this is simply clever psychology, you may retort, after all, most people would struggle with the inner conflict of unfinished business. And you may have a point. But for the sake of self-reflection, humour me for a moment. On a scale of 1-10 (10 being the highest point of achievement and 1 being the lowest) how would you score yourself on your purpose chart?

Do you feel you've accomplished half of what you were created to do in this life? How about a quarter? Or would you score yourself below a 3? Could it be that amidst the hustle and bustle of your busy life, you've shelved your life's mission?

KNOCK KNOCK

Now if you're anything like me, living a mundane, mediocre life would be almost as morbid as not living at all. Deep down, you've always believed that there was more to your life than meets the eye. Nevertheless, you keep catching yourself (more often than you care to admit) procrastinating and putting off your destiny. You keep filling up your time with pointless pursuits.

But every now and then, Destiny shows up. And when He does, we all respond so differently. In those rare moments when destiny gently knocks our door, some of us will pretend to be out. Others will busy themselves with silly things to avoid answering. They'll do the vacuuming, surf the net, spring clean, watch reality TV — you name it.

Once in a while, the more curious among us may peer out

from behind the curtain of our comfort zones. But the really bold among us, may go as far as cracking the door open a smidgen, and barking out the question: 'What do *you* want?'

But what if we each found the courage to open that door, and fully embrace the truth of what we were created to do in life?

PERFECT TIMING

Like the first time a fledgling eagle takes to the sky; or a young lioness makes her first kill, you'll know the moment destiny steps through your door. From the moment you begin to take tentative steps towards your life's assignment, something unusual will happen: you'll begin to see what God sees when He looks at you!

Ideas like firework displays, will begin to light up your mind. You'll be awoken to the edgier, less predictable side of your personality. Parts of your life that you saw as crude pieces of a pointless patchwork, will suddenly unfold before you like a masterpiece.

Your gifts. Your passions. Your idiosyncrasies. Even the most painful ordeals that you've gone through in life, these will all fuse together to form a fascinating curriculum vitae. Things that used to impede and intimidate you will seem silly and inconsequential. A confidence you've never known before, will be birthed in you. And you will resolve in your heart that for you, failure is no longer an option.

As we bring this chapter to a close, I encourage you to be as honest with yourself as you can. If you've been spending time on fruitless pursuits, and if you've been finding excuses not to embrace your destiny, then it's time to make some changes. The Chinese have a saying: *If you find yourself in a hole, stop digging!* Perhaps the worst kind of hole you or I can find ourselves in, is one of our own making. So, no more excuses ... no more delays. Here are 7 powerful facts about procrastination:

1. Procrastination undermines your ability to prosper in life.

The lazy man will not plow because of winter; He will beg during harvest and have nothing. (Proverbs 20:4 NKJV).

2. Procrastination denies you first place in life.

The hand of the diligent will rule, But the lazy man will be put to forced labor. (Proverbs 12:24 NKJV).

3. Procrastination makes you forfeit God's blessings.

Therefore take the talent from him, and give it to him who has ten talents. (Matthew 25:28 NKJV).

4. Procrastination will make you miss your mission

I must work the works of Him who sent Me while it is day; the night is coming when no one can work. (John 9:4 NKJV).

5. Procrastination makes you miss out on opportunities.

And while they went to buy, the bridegroom came, and those who were ready went in with him to the wedding; and the door was shut. (Matthew 25:10 NKJV).

6. Procrastination leads to idleness, and idleness opens the door to temptation.

*It happened in the spring of the year, at the time when kings go out to battle, that David sent Joab and his servants with him, and all Israel; and they destroyed the people of Ammon and besieged Rabbah. <u>**But David remained at Jerusalem.**</u> Then it happened one evening that David arose from his bed and walked on the roof of the king's house. And from the roof he saw a woman bathing, and the woman was very beautiful to behold.*
(2 Samuel 11:1-2 emphasis mine NKJV).

7. Procrastination leads to indecision, confusion and frustration.

... he is a double-minded man, unstable in all his ways.
(James 1:8 NKJV).

Points To Ponder ...

- Write down 3 major projects that you keep putting off.
- What difference would it make to your life if you accomplished these 3 things?
- Make a list of 3 things that distract you the most. Try consciously removing these distractions from your life over the next 3 months. You may be surprised by the results.

Prayer Time

Dear Lord, thank you for the plans that you have carefully laid out for my life. According to Jeremiah 29:11, these plans guarantee a place of significance in this world. Lord, I come to you today because I am determined not to miss out on my mission. Please help me manage my time more effectively. Please grant me the discipline to complete all of my divine assignments. By faith, I declare that:

- *I am no longer apathetic about the future (John 9:4).*

- *I am no longer anxious about the future (Ecclesiastes 3:11).*

- *I am no longer confused about the future (Psalms 37:23).*

- *I am no longer dreading the future (Psalms 42:11).*

- *My life is now synchronised with heaven's timetable, and I cannot fail (Ecclesiastes 3:1) Amen.*

CHAPTER 11

PRIDE

God resists the proud, but gives grace to the humble

– Peter The Apostle

FACT: GOD RESISTS arrogant people. Plainly put, those who walk in arrogance — ill-treating the downtrodden, and the vulnerable — are picking a fight with God! Now why on earth would you want to do *that*? Life's tough enough as it is. Anyone who's had to claw their way into each meaningful moment in their life, will know exactly what I mean! So when the attacks coming against you aren't demonic or hell-sent, but the result of heaven's resistance against you … *you're in trouble!* Consider the following cases:

1. Adam's plight of having to suffer and sweat for a living, wasn't the result of an assignment from hell — it was God's doing:

And to the man he said, "Since you listened to your wife and ate from the tree whose fruit I commanded you not to eat, the ground is cursed because of you. All your life you will struggle to scratch a living from it. (Genesis 3:17 NLT).

2. Cain's crippling life-sentence banishing him from the presence and provision of the Lord, wasn't Satan's verdict — but the Lord's:

No longer will the ground yield good crops for you,
no matter how hard you work! From now on you will be a
homeless wanderer on the earth." (Genesis 4:12 NLT).

**3. The storm that almost destroyed Jonah and a ship's
entire crew, wasn't a product of the occult. It wasn't the
result of spooky spells or incantations, it was the
outcome of the fight he'd picked with God:**
But the Lord hurled a powerful wind over the sea, causing a
violent storm that threatened to break the ship apart.
(Jonah 1:4 NLT).

SAY IT LOUD I'M BLACK-HEARTED AND PROUD

So why *does* the Lord hate pride so much? The answer is
revealed in the following scripture references: Isaiah 14:12-
17, Ezekiel 28:12-19, Luke 10:18, Revelation 12:3-4.

Lucifer, we are told, was once one of the most beautiful
angels in heaven. Gifted and bedecked with rare stones, he
possessed a special anointing for service in the courts of
heaven. Now, we know that gem stones are highly prized
for their beauty and ability to reflect light. If Lucifer was
bedecked with precious stones, we can safely conclude that
his true value lay in his ability to reflect God's glory. Instead,
we're told that he began to incubate a nasty little pathogen
named pride in the secret recesses of his heart. Fostering a
desire to be worshipped, Lucifer strutted into the throne
room, and tried to overthrow God's sovereignty. The result?

An epic hammering!

> *Then there was war in heaven. Michael and his angels fought against the dragon and his angels. And the dragon lost the battle, and he and his angels were forced out of heaven. This great dragon — the ancient serpent called the devil, or Satan, the one deceiving the whole world — was thrown down to the earth with all his angels.*
> — Revelation 12:7-9 NLT

PRIDE AND PREJUDICE

Pride is a modern form of idolatry. It is the worship of self. It is to place one's self above everyone and everything else. Those operating in this kind of conceit are poisoning their own progress in life.

To walk in arrogance, one must make all sorts of hideous prejudgements about others — hence the word prejudice. Pride causes you to see yourself towering above those around you. It makes you try to dominate every environment that you enter into.

Pride is a pathogen that will make others sick of the sight of you. As it stands, the pride pandemic that's broken out in the 21st century, has infected millions. Like a scene out of Marc Forster's *World War Z*, millions of glassy-eyed individuals roam the earth spreading their self-seeking, self-absorbed, sickness. Does the world really *need* one more pride-zombie? Why not let your life be the antidote? Why not join the handful of humble warriors committed to eradicating this social epidemic?

The sad fact is that an individual infected with pride, can

hardly ever utter the words: 'I am sorry.' I've seen marriages destroyed, churches shut down, businesses lost, souls crushed, and lives lost as a result of pride. And so, as we approach the conclusion of this chapter, I would like to leave you with 7 powerful facts about pride.

1. The Lord hates pride. Remember, it was the first sin.

Everyone proud in heart is an abomination to the Lord; Though they join forces, none will go unpunished (Proverbs 16:5 NKJV).

2. Pride depletes the grace, favour and mercy of God from our lives.

Likewise you younger people, submit yourselves to your elders. Yes, all of you be submissive to one another, and be clothed with humility, for "God resists the proud, But gives grace to the humble." (1 Peter 5:5 emphasis mine NKJV).

3. Pride opens the door to deception.

The pride of your heart has deceived you,
You who dwell in the clefts of the rock,
Whose habitation is high; You who say in your heart,
'Who will bring me down to the ground?' (Obadiah 1:3 NKJV)

4. Pride causes us to drift from God.

The wicked in his proud countenance does not seek God;
God is in none of his thoughts. (Psalms 10:4 NKJV)

5.Pride guarantees failure.

Pride goes before destruction, And a haughty spirit before a fall. (Proverbs 16:18 NKJV)

6.Pride leads to spiritual bondage.

Therefore pride serves as their necklace; Violence covers them like a garment. (Psalms 73:6 NKJV)

7.Pride destroys relationships.

By pride comes nothing but strife, But with the well-advised is wisdom. (Proverbs 13:10 NKJV).

Remember, pride pollutes purpose!

Points To Ponder ...

- Has the Lord ever needed to humble you in the past?
- What are the types of circumstances/scenarios that usually promote or produce arrogance in you?
- List three things that you can do to help guard against pride and arrogance.

Prayer Time

Dear Lord, thank you for your grace. Thank you for your constant kindness and gentleness towards me. I recognise now, how subtly the pathogen of pride can enter into one's heart, and I confess that at times, I too have yielded to its stealthy approach. I repent for those times when I have been prideful and have allowed my ego to cut-and-paste my agendas over your wishes. By faith, I now declare that:

- *I am no longer operating in the domain of pride (2 Chronicles 7:14).*

- *I am free from all self-centred agendas (2 Chronicles 34:27).*

- *I am clothed with the humility of Jesus Christ (Matthew 11:29).*

- *I am a recipient of the grace of God (James 4:6).*

- *I am a blessing and a breath of fresh air to those I encounter (Matthew 5:14) Amen.*

CHAPTER 12

IMMORALITY

The Bible will keep you from sin, or sin will keep you
from the Bible.

– Dwight L. Moody

IF PRIDE WAS a pathogen, then sin (immorality) would
be the first sign of its sickness. Sin sedates the soul and
numbs one's conscience to the will of God. The sin-sickness
starts out like little lesions on the soul that soon fester into
full-blown ulcers, with the power to put one's destiny in
the grave:

> *Then, when desire has conceived, it gives birth to sin;
> and sin, when it is full-grown, brings forth death.*
>
> — James 1:15 NKJV

Some call it bad karma. Some call it negative energy — or bad
vibes. I've even heard village communities in Africa (where I
come from) refer to it as 'upsetting the ancestors'. But however
people attempt to explain this strange phenomenon, it seems
to be a universally accepted truth: what goes around, comes
around! Whether you see the fruit of your choices/actions
today or a decade from now, very few refute the existence of
a cosmic law guaranteeing a harvest for every seed sown —
good or bad.

Now when I speak of sin, please don't try to picture me

standing on some kind of soap box with a bony finger pointed in the air and flecks of spittle flying from my mouth. I promise you, I'm not mentally trapped in the dark ages with my head buried in the sand. I'm a 21st century preacher. I understand the debates surrounding postmodernism and Christianity. I appreciate that times change, societies move on, and bigots become extinct. I am a progressive Christian, but having said all that, I still believe that sin is sin! William Shakespeare once wrote:

> What's in a name? That which we call a rose By any other name would smell as sweet.
>
> — Juliet Capulet Act II, Scene II

Hey guys, you can gift-wrap it, put pretty lace ribbons on it, surround it with cuddly toys and slap Chanel no 5 on the thing ... but sin still stinks! Immorality still offends heaven and remains one of the biggest catalysts for wholesale destruction on earth (Proverbs 14: 34).

Sin corrodes the soul. It bores tiny holes in your character— sometimes without any immediate or notable consequences. Sin reminds me of the creature from Ridley Scott's movie: *Alien*. I remember watching that film for the first time and wondering why anybody would want to leave the safety of their spaceship to walk headlong into a nightmare. For those of you who are unfamiliar with the storyline, here's a quick synopsis.

The crew of the Nostromo (a commercial spaceship) picks up an unknown signal from a tiny planet on their way back to earth, and decide to investigate. When they land on the planetoid, three crew members, Dallas, Kane and Lambert disembark and begin to explore. Now, at this point, the music score changes to that why-would-you-even-contemplate-going-any-further kind of music. They discover a derelict alien spaceship. There is some kind of dead, fossilised creature in this alien craft, and a huge hole in the floor. Too curious to quit now, Kane is lowered into the hole where he discovers a hive colony of egg-like pods.

Steam. A misty green light. Kane is fixated. He thinks he sees something moving in one of the pods.

'Get away from there MAN!' I shriek at the screen, but Kane is far too engrossed to hear me. He flashes a light at the pod and the outline of a spider-like creature is vividly illuminated.

'Kane, I beg you ... please leave!' I try again. But Kane goes all 'gangsta' on me and draws his pistol. The top of the pod pops open. Kane can't help himself, he does the unmentionable. He pushes his face into the pod for a better look! The creature shoots out (surprise surprise) and attaches itself to his neck-back ... I mean — helmet! *Now* the thing has him in a vice-like grip.

When they carry poor Kane back to the ship and remove his helmet, they are horrified to discover that the alien parasite has inserted a tube-like appendage into his throat and is feeding him oxygen. *It's keeping him alive for it's own sinister purpose!*

Hours pass, and suddenly the creature dislodges itself from Kane's face, and dies. To everyone's joy and amazement, Kane rejoins the rest of the crew seemingly unaffected. Suddenly though, as he sits eating his first meal since the 'incident', he begins to choke and convulse violently. Bursting out of his chest cavity, is a little snake-like creature that screeches at the top of its voice and scurries off out of sight. Then the nightmare truly begins.

SOUL SURVIVOR

They hatch vipers' eggs and weave the spider's web;
He who eats of their eggs dies, And from that which is
crushed a viper breaks out.

— Isaiah 59:5 NKJV

Immorality starts out in exactly the same way. It can spring at you from a TV/computer screen. It can leap off the pages of a book. It can even travel through the touch of the wrong person at the wrong time. Like Ridley Scott's alien parasite, sin will clamp itself to your mind, insert its appendages into your imagination and lay eggs in your spirit. And just like in the movie, sin loves to feign death. You'll sigh a huge sigh of relief, enjoying a moment's reprieve. But when all seems calm and back to normal, something will start to move on the inside of you. At first, like Kane, you'll just boil it down to bad indigestion: *I knew that pizza looked suspect!* But when you suddenly turn pale, break out into a cold sweat, and start staggering around clutching at your guts, the truth will finally hit you: *sin's on the inside of you … and it's trying to kill you!*

I call it *alien*, because it may be something that's not even a part of the real you. Something that you actually hate doing. Something that leaves you baffled as to why you're even doing it. For some, the sin-alien may be the need for the next high. For others, it may be the pull of perverse sexual inclinations. Anger, blame, jealousy, hatred, greed, gambling, manipulation

— these are just a few of the festering pods waiting for the next host.

Now I know that Kane ignored me, but I'm praying that I'll have more success with you. Whatever 'festering pods' you've been prodding at and 'investigating' lately, please think again. It's time to leave that sin bin behind — *while you still can!*

As we reach the end of this chapter, let's consider 4 interesting facts about sin:

1. Sin empowers the enemy to attack you.

He who digs a pit will fall into it, And whoever breaks through a wall will be bitten by a serpent. (Ecclesiastes 10:8 NKJV).

2. Sin keeps the Lord from helping you.

If I regard iniquity in my heart, The Lord will not hear. (Psalms 66:18 NKJV)

Behold, the Lord's hand is not shortened, That it cannot save; Nor His ear heavy, That it cannot hear. But your iniquities have separated you from your God; And your sins have hidden His face from you, So that He will not hear. (Isaiah 59:1-2 NKJV)

3. Sin is a savage form of self-harming.

Whoever commits adultery with a woman lacks understanding; He who does so destroys his own soul. (Proverbs 6:32 NKJV)

Then, when desire has conceived, it gives birth to sin; and sin, when it is full-grown, brings forth death. (James 1:15 NKJV)

4. Sin will make you forfeit your place in heaven.

But there shall by no means enter it anything that defiles, or causes an abomination or a lie, but only those who are written in the Lamb's Book of Life. (Revelation 21:27 NKJV)

Points To Ponder ...

- What are your top 3 non-negotiable principals in life?
- Have you ever wandered off from the 'safe ground' of these principals?
- Identify 3 temptations that you need to walk away from today.

Prayer Time

Dear Lord, thank you for your amazing grace. By faith, I stand on your promise that if I confess my sins and immoral thoughts/actions you will forgive me (1John1:9). I acknowledge and repent of my public and private sins. These include ——————————
Lord, through Your divine authority, I now declare that:

- *Sin no longer has any dominion over any area of my life (Romans 6:14).*

- *I'm released from every physical, emotional or spiritual contamination that has resulted through my own immoral choices/actions. (Psalms 103:12).*

- *I release God's fire on every demonic colony seeking to establish itself in my life. (Psalms 97:3).*

- *Every demonic personality attaching itself to my psyche, is destroyed right now (Isaiah 54:17) Amen.*

CHAPTER 13

GUILT

They whose guilt within their bosom lies, imagine every eye
beholds their blame.

– William Shakespeare

GUILT IS LIKE a mind-altering drug. It will distort everything that you see and hear, turning them into ear-piercing accusations. It'll play tricks on your mind and paralyse you with paranoia. When you're guilt-ridden, you become a mere parody of yourself. Instead of having an upright posture and a twinkle in your eye, you're reduced to hunched shoulders and a perpetual apology to the whole world.

Guilt is another one of Satan's secret weapons. He has used it over the aeons to strip prophets of their prophesies, and rob worshippers of their melodies. Wielding it like a wrecking ball, he uses it to smash his way through the confidence of his victims. Then he sets about moulding them into hell's most valuable asset: the self-harmer. Night and day they'll sit slashing themselves with jagged memories from the past (Mark 5:5).

Of all the 'destiny killers' out there, guilt is perhaps one of the most lethal because it moves like an assassin. You won't see it coming. It can sneak past the scriptures in your mind, and abseil down the walls of your convictions. It can dart around in the shadows of your vulnerable moments, and pounce on you as soon as you're alone. And like any trained killer, guilt is always armed with an arsenal of formidable weapons. Just one word. One thought. One hypnotic suggestion, and its victims are soon brow-beaten into a posture of defeat.

GUILT TRIP TO NOWHERE

Guilt's true success however, depends almost entirely on its victim. For guilt to have it's wicked way with us, we have to allow ourselves to be caught by its lasso of lies. We have to allow ourselves to be bundled off into its 'dodgy old van' — and taken on a trip. A guilt trip. I've been on lots of those. The last guilt trip I went on lasted half a lifetime. It gave me ample time to take in all the sights. Please take my word for it when I tell you that the trip's a complete scam. It isn't worth a micro-moment of your time!

My trip began in a God-forsaken village called *Accusation*. The dirty old banger of a tour bus, just kept taking me round and round the same old ruins of my past failures. Finally, I was taken on a perverse little pilgrimage to the unholy lands: self-reproach, self-loathing, and self-annihilation. By the time I came back from the tour, I wanted to kill myself!

Now, unless this sounds like the kind of place you've always longed to visit, I implore you to burn all your 'guilt brochures' now! **Guilt is not your destination.**

Perhaps, as you sat reading this chapter, it began to occur to you that you're stuck on a similar trip right now. The symptoms are easy enough to spot.

1. You can hardly pray.

Each time you stand to pray, you feel yourself wilting on the inside. You feel as though you can hardly bring yourself to talk to the Lord because of whatever it is you've done.

2. You suffer with low self-esteem and a poor self-image.

You have little self-confidence, and the slightest hint of disapproval or criticism from anyone, sends you free falling into a world of paranoia. You've become so sensitive that those around you have to walk on egg shells.

3. You feel unworthy to fulfil your life's purpose.

You consider it highly unlikely that the Lord will ever rely on you for His missions. In fact, you sometimes feel as though the Lord has moved on from you because of your 'issues'.

4. You feel hopeless about the future.

Your negative thoughts are like a broken record; and most of the time you just feel drained. Where your aspirations once burned, there now stands a derelict hearth with the ashes of yesteryear smouldering inside it.

Dear friend, it's important to recognise that the lord isn't like you and I. He said so Himself:

> *"My thoughts are nothing like your thoughts," says the Lord. "And my ways are far beyond anything you could imagine.*
>
> — Isaiah 55:8 NLT

When someone offends us, we find it difficult to forgive them and move on. We struggle because we're human, and the fear of them doing it again, creates 'trust issues' in our hearts.

It's even worse when the said offences were completely unprovoked or unjustified. We try to forgive them, but the moment we see them, something like a fist clenches in the pit of our stomachs. Our smile becomes tight, and our body language becomes tense. And if we're suddenly thrust into a conversation with them, we tilt our heads and nod politely — but our minds have already left the building! Basically, we just want distance — preferably continental — between us and the 'Judas' in question.

The Lord is different though. Impaled to the cross, He felt sorry for those who were butchering Him ...

He prayed for them (Luke 23:34). He could have dismounted from the cross and fast-tracked them all to hell. But His love for you and I kept Him pinned there. The thought of us made Him submit to torture. Like the *Saw* horror movies, He was given a melancholy choice: avoid the agony of the cross, or bear the pain of seeing you and I go to hell. And so, like any passionate parent, He found a way to set His children free.

So my friend, if the brutality of the cross couldn't stop Him from loving you, be assured of this one thing: nothing ever could. No matter what you've done; no matter how ashamed you feel; Jesus made up His mind to *always* love you.

NOT GUILTY

So, never allow your life to become a courtroom drama. Some of the folks you meet along the way will assume the role of prosecutor in your life. They'll try to accuse you of everything under the sun and expect you to defend your actions 24/7. Some may try to become self-appointed jurors. But I warn you now, some of the really deluded ones, may even try to approach you as judge, juror and executioner all rolled into one! But there is only one true Judge. He alone has the power to judge you. He presides over the high courts of heaven, and His verdict on earth is final. The minute you confess your sins to Him, His not-guilty verdict over you will be irrevocable:

> *Forever, O Lord, Your word is settled in heaven.*
> — Psalms 119:89 NKJV

Finally, some helpful facts about guilt:

1. Once your sins are confessed to the Lord, He wipes the slate clean.
But if we confess our sins to him, he is faithful and just to forgive us our sins and to cleanse us from all wickedness. (1John1:9 NKJV)

2. Forgiving you makes the Lord happy.
"I—yes, I alone—will blot out your sins for my own sake and will never think of them again. (Isaiah 43:25 NKJV)

3. God's presence in your life goes beyond your actions.
If I ascend into heaven, You are there; If I make my bed in hell, behold, You are there. (Psalms 139:8 NKJV)

4. The Lord won't make you jump through hoops for His forgiveness.

Then he said to Jesus, "Lord, remember me when You come into Your kingdom." And Jesus said to him, "Assuredly, I say to you, today you will be with Me in Paradise." (Luke 23: 42-43 NKJV).

Points To Ponder ...

- Write 3 things down on a sheet of paper (preferably one that self-destructs later) that you've done in your life that you're utterly ashamed of.
- How would you feel if you never had to squirm about those issues ever again?
- Do you believe that your sins and indiscretions are unprecedented? Or is it possible that the Lord has seen and forgiven greater sins than yours?

Prayer Time

Dear Lord, thank you for loving me. Thank you for forgiving me. And thank you for wiping my sin-slate clean. By faith, I stand on your gracious promise that with Jesus in my life, no one can condemn me (Romans 8:1). Through your divine authority, I now declare that:

- *I have been forgiven (1 John 1:9).*
- *I am no longer imprisoned by guilt (Romans 5:1).*
- *All who try to judge me run the risk of being condemned themselves (Isaiah 54:17).*
- *Every demonic personality attacking my mind with guilt, is destroyed right now in the name of Jesus (Isaiah 54:17) Amen.*

CHAPTER 14

IGNORANCE

Fool me once, shame on you, fool me twice, shame on me

– Anonymous

IGNORANCE IS A crippling disability. It's a form of mind blindness. When your mind is blind, you'll end up falling into one of life's many ditches. Social ditches. Spiritual ditches. Financial ditches. Relational ditches. And the sad thing about it is that when you're mentally sightless, no sooner than you're out of one crisis, you'll find yourself tumbling into another.

Now it's true that when a person has an impairment of some sort in one area, they may become extremely advanced in others. The visually impaired, for instance, may develop an extraordinary sense of hearing. The physically restricted (like the physicist Stephen Hawkins) may become academically awe-inspiring etc. Being the masters of survival that we are, we usually come up with clever ways to compensate for the 'less endowed' areas of our lives.

But no matter how ingenious or intuitive our cover-up campaigns are, we always get 'busted' in the end. Someone always manages to uncover our 'little secrets'.

GRIN AND BEAR IT

I remember when I first arrived in England. Although I was born in Shrewsbury, my family and I had moved to Nigeria when I was 6 years old. I didn't return to the UK until I was 12. Having missed out on so much Western education, I felt like a prized Muppet every time I opened my mouth. For me, class discussions were like being thrown to the lions!

'So Michael,' my teacher once asked, taking great pains to include me in all the deliberations. 'What contributions would you have liked to have made during the renaissance?' As all eyes zoomed in on me, I just sat there gawking like Black Bean (the black Mr Bean). My ingenious strategy of grinning and nodding at every word (whether I understood it or not) could only take me so far! And now, these people were actually expecting some kind of response from me: *God help me!*

The moment I opened my mouth (which by now was drier than the Sahara desert) I knew it was a mistake. My accent sealed my doom. I sounded like Kunta Kinte on amphetamines! I might as well have stepped off the banana boat that very morning for all the sense I made. Unintentionally, I became the most entertaining character in class — but for all the wrong reasons.

CONQUERING MT. STUPID

Now, being laughed at in life can result in one of two outcomes:

a) You can become bitter and chronically defensive.

b)You can become better and resolve to improve yourself.

Thankfully, I chose the latter. From that day forth, I vowed to conquer Mt. Stupid.

I began to amass all the mountain-climbing gear that I could find. A backpack full of encyclopedias. An ice axe in the form of the Oxford Dictionary. And a climbing harness that took the form of a library membership. Equipped to the hilt, I began my scrambling ascent to the summit of my mountain. In my heart, I vowed to plant a big, bright, flag when I got to the top. This flag would have the words: *I'm no longer a moron!* emblazoned on it. Well, that was the plan anyway.

The very first thing that I needed to do, was rid myself of my accent. Disclaimer! I would like to go on record here and clearly state that there is absolutely nothing wrong with the Nigerian accent. But sounding like the Nigerian version of a pre-pubescent Shaka Zulu (in an all-white school) did nothing for my 'flow'. So I'd sit listening to Radio 4 in the evenings, practising the tight-lipped phonetic pronunciations of its broadcasters.

Finally, my hard work paid off. Shaka was exorcised, and I began to speak with a half-decent English lilt.

Around this time, I also began to read ceaselessly. I read everything from Reader's Digest to Nietzsche; from Mills & Boon to The Acts Of The Apostles. In time, I began to scale my way to the summit of that dreaded mountain.

IN THE KNOW

If you don't climb the mountain you can't see the view
— Anonymous

Once I reached the summit of my mountain, the view up there was spectacular. The new perspectives that I gained from reading was like standing back and watching fire-work displays for the first time. My mind became a screen upon which the Holy Spirit could start projecting 'Power Point' presentations of my future. Incredibly, I began to perceive new abilities within myself. Through my little 'excursion' into different subjects, I discovered that:

- I had a vivid imagination
- I had excellent retention skills
- I was a good orator/communicator
- I was a writer
- I had a flair for music

TREASURE HUNT

You see, beneath the wreckage of our fears and insecurities, lies a gold mine. A reservoir of unique gifts waiting to be unearthed. Once excavated, these abilities can be carefully refined and polished until they begin to sparkle.

But you have to *see* it before you can *seize* it. From the moment that you make a conscious decision to enrich, expand and enlarge your knowledge base, something extraordinary will begin to happen to you. You will begin to unearth your true passions. And your passions will leave footprints to your purpose. Finally, here are 5 interesting facts about knowledge/ignorance.

1. Ignorance is destructive.

My people are destroyed for lack of knowledge ...(Hosea 4:6 NKJV)

2. Ignorance places limits on your life.

Therefore my people have gone into captivity, because they have no knowledge ... (Isaiah 5:13 NKJV)

3. Ignorance attracts self-imposed difficulties.

A fool's proud talk becomes a rod that beats him, but the words of the wise keep them safe. (Proverbs 14:3 NLT)

4. Knowledge opens doors.

Then Pharaoh said to Joseph, "Since God has revealed the meaning of the dreams to you, clearly no one else is as intelligent or wise as you are. You will be in charge of my court, and all my people will take orders from you. Only I, sitting on my throne, will have a rank higher than yours." Pharaoh said to Joseph, "I hereby put you in charge of the entire land of Egypt." (Genesis 41: 39-41 NLT)

5. Knowledge brings stability.

Wisdom and knowledge will be the stability of your times ... (Isaiah 33:6 NKJV)

Remember: knowledge is power!

Points To Ponder ...

- Have you ever been embarrassed by your lack of knowledge in a specific area?

- Doctors, dentists, mechanics, lawyers: all are paid for their expertise. There is an undeniable correlation between one's knowledge base, and their value to others. What's *your* area of expertise?

- Make a list with 3 columns. In the first, list your gifts, qualities, and abilities. If you find yourself struggling, enlist the help of someone whose opinion you trust. In the second column, list your passions. Finally, in the third, list your areas of expertise. How well do the columns match up? Repeat this simple exercise every 6 months or so, until you begin to see a consistency across the columns.

Prayer Time

Dear Lord, You give sight to the sightless, and you heal mind-blindness. Thank you for covering me during those times when ignorance could have destroyed me. I was 'styling it out' but You were breaking me out! You blessed me with the learning tools to put an end to my drought. Thank you for advancing me in life. I pray that You will grant me the will and discipline to study (2 Timothy 2:15).

As I continue on my quest for knowledge, I declare that:

- *I have the mind of Christ (Philippians 2:5).*

- *My relationship with God forms the foundation of my education. (Proverbs 1:7).*

- *My quest for knowledge and understanding will be divinely rewarded (Proverbs 18:15-16).*

- *The knowledge that I acquire from now on, will be the kind that enriches my soul. (Proverbs 8:10). Amen.*

PART III
THE UNLEASHING

STEPPING OUT

ON

PURPOSE

... For this cause I was born, and for this cause I have come into the world ...

John 18:37 NKJV

CHAPTER 15

BACK TO THE FUTURE

Freedom is not worth having if it does not include the
freedom to make mistakes.

– Mahatma Gandhi

I F YOU COULD travel back in time and meet a younger
version of yourself, what kind of conversation would
you have? Would you sit your younger self down and
calmly impart your pearls of wisdom? Or would you just
grab yourself by the lapels and blurt out as many warnings
as you could before you were sucked back into time's
meandering corridor?

Personally, I'd take myself off on a lovely retreat. Mmmm ...
somewhere nice. Somewhere quiet and secluded, with
absolutely no distractions at all. Then I'd give myself a good
hiding! Seriously. I'd drop-kick that brother into another
time zone. Finally, I'd execute a few ninjutsu moves on him,
and tap him out (MMA style!).

Now I know that my statements may seem a little odd
(disturbing even), but perhaps once I've explained, you'll find
yourself nodding in agreement. You see, after 44 years on this
earth, I've discovered an unavoidable, irrefutable truth:

**MY LIFE TODAY IS THE SUM TOTAL OF MY
CHOICES YESTERDAY.**

- Precious moments wasted ...
- Opportunities not taken ...
- Talents left unused ...
- Potential left unplumbed ...
- The scores of fruitless relationships ...
- The charlatans that fooled me ...
- The impostors that intimidated me ...

All of the above, were either directly or indirectly the fruit of my own reckless, or uninformed choices. I had no idea that *Yesterday* was pregnant with my *Today*. But the God that I serve is a good God! He is the God of second chances, and helped me recognise (while there was still time) that my *Today* is also pregnant with my *Tomorrow!* He helped me see that I still possess the power of choice.

Each time I make a choice, a creative force with the power to produce a change, is released. I am made in the express image of my heavenly Father (Genesis 1:26, John 10:34-35). This means that when I say 'let there be ...', *there simply is!*

Through the creative power of choice, I realised that I don't have to live my life in the purgatory of remorse and regrets. I don't have to limp around in a labyrinth of lies, feeling that everyone is superior to me. But most important of all, I don't have to live my life in a pantomime, where every Tom, Dick and Harry gets to join in on the call-and-response chants:

"Michael Ekwulugo is blessed!"

"Oh no he isn't!"

"Oh yes he is…" and so forth.

The Lord has given me editorial control over my life through the vehicle of my choices and decisions. He has empowered me with the unique ability to define my future:

> Today I have given you the choice between life and death, between blessings and curses. Now I call on heaven and earth to witness the choice you make. Oh, that you would choose life, so that you and your descendants might live!
>
> — Deuteronomy 30:19 NLT

A LITTLE LETTER TO MYSELF

So, although there are times when I'd like to blame society, my parentage, my race, social injustices, and the price of bananas in the banana republics, for my struggles in life — the truth is that I can find no other culprit than the man in the mirror. I think Michael Jackson was having a prophetic moment!

Therefore, given the opportunity to travel back in time and make radical changes to history, I wouldn't tamper with government institutions, global economy, or even critical issues like bringing mango milkshakes back to McDonald's (Kiss teeth!! It was just a promotion ☹).

No. My only mission would be erasing the foolishness from my earlier mindsets.

Now, because I couldn't be sure of the length of time I'd have with myself, I would need to be clear, clinical, and concise with my instructions. I think I'd write a little letter to myself. It would go something like this …

Dear younger Michael,

First of all, sorry for the black eye! I don't know what came over me. Anyway Mike, what's done is done. So, now that I've finally got your undivided attention, please let me share the following wisdom keys with you.

1. Your *tomorrow* is carried in the womb of your *today*. As you make choices today, always make them with tomorrow in view. Never let the emotions of the moment cloud your judgement. Never make choices today that you can't stand by tomorrow. Always make choices with eternity in view.

> *Don't be misled — you cannot mock the justice of God. You will always harvest what you plant. Those who live only to satisfy their own sinful nature will harvest decay and death from that sinful nature. But those who live to please the Spirit will harvest everlasting life from the Spirit.*
>
> — Galatians 6:7-8 NLT

> *They have planted the wind and will harvest the whirlwind.*
>
> — Hosea 8:7 NLT

> *Those who plant in tears will harvest with shouts of joy. They weep as they go to plant their seed, but they sing as they return with the harvest.*
>
> — Psalms 126:5-6 NLT

2. Falling isn't failing.

When you fall (note that I didn't say if) try to fall forward! A failed attempt at something can be the best 'instruction manual' for your next attempt. Failure teaches you what not to do, and breaks down the anatomy of success for you. Make sure that your failed attempts leave you better and not bitter. Failure is not falling — true failure is being too afraid to get up again. Remember: your attitude determines your aptitude.

> *The godly may trip seven times, but they will get up again. But one disaster is enough to overthrow the wicked.*
> — Proverbs 24:16 NLT

> *The Lord directs the steps of the godly.*
> *He delights in every detail of their lives.*
> *Though they stumble, they will never fall,*
> *for the Lord holds them by the hand.*
> — Psalms 37:23-24 NLT

> *And we know that God causes everything to work together for the good of those who love God and are called according to his purpose for them.*
> — Romans 8:28 NLT

3. If you keep rehearsing it, you'll keep reversing it.

If you keep going over old hurts, you'll keep reliving the effects of them. Letting go of an offence and choosing to forgive the offender, breaks the power of the past. The secret to being happy is learning to distance yourself from the things that make you sad.

*If another believer sins, rebuke that person; then
if there is repentance, forgive. Even if that person
wrongs you seven times a day and each time turns
again and asks forgiveness, you must forgive.*
— Luke 17:3-4 NLT

*Then Peter came to him and asked, "Lord, how often
should I forgive someone who sins against me?
Seven times?" "No, not seven times," Jesus replied, "but
seventy times seven!*
— Matthew 18:21-22 NLT

4. Turn your weakness into a weapon.

Resist the temptation of trying to hide your weaknesses.
Take the time to identify your 'Achilles heel' before your
enemies do. Working on your weak points will ultimately
make you sharper, stronger and less vulnerable.

*...First get rid of the log in your own eye; then you
will see well enough to deal with the speck in your
friend's eye.*
— Matthew 7:5 NLT

*He looked around at them one by one and then said
to the man, "Hold out your hand." So the man held
out his hand, and it was restored!*
— Luke 6:10 NLT

*Each time he said, "My grace is all you need. My
power works best in weakness." So now I am glad
to boast about my weaknesses, so that the power
of Christ can work through me.*
— 2 Corinthians 12:9 NLT

5. Be kind to yourself

There's an old African proverb that says, 'If there's no enemy within, the enemy outside can do us no harm'. Learn to be at peace with yourself. World War Me is a pointless war: both sides loose in the end. Friendly fire isn't friendly: it's deadly. So, be careful not to entertain the enemy-in-me.

> *Now David was greatly distressed, for the people spoke of stoning him, because the soul of all the people was grieved, every man for his sons and his daughters.* **But David strengthened himself in the Lord his God.**
>
> — 1 Samuel 30:6 (emphasis mine) NKJV

> *You must love the Lord your God with all your heart, all your soul, all your strength, and all your mind. And,* **Love your neighbour as yourself.**
>
> — Luke 10:27 (emphasis mine) NKJV

6. Don't give up, don't give in — give everything.

Acceptance of conditions that you cannot change, is the key to contentment. Learning to rewrite your expectations, can give you fresh perspectives as well as give your creativity a boost. Remember: no condition is permanent. Things that seem like stumbling blocks today, may turn out to be stepping stones to a better place tomorrow. So no matter how despondent you may feel always remind yourself that there is no life so impaired that it cannot be repaired!

> *Weeping may last through the night, but joy comes with the morning.*
>
> — Psalms 30:5b NLT

The godly may trip seven times, but they will get up again. But one disaster is enough to overthrow the wicked.

— Proverbs 24:16 NLT

I know how to live on almost nothing or with everything. I have learned the secret of living in every situation, whether it is with a full stomach or empty, with plenty or little. For I can do everything through Christ, who gives me strength.

— Philippians 4:12-13 NLT

7. Always have an attitude of gratitude.

Never allow the blessings you desire, to eclipse the blessings you've acquired. It requires the same amount of mental energy to generate negative thoughts as it does positive ones. Be thankful for what you've got and consider how blessed you are.

Don't worry about anything; instead, pray about everything. Tell God what you need, and thank him for all he has done.

— Philippians 4:6 NLT

Be thankful in all circumstances, for this is God's will for you who belong to Christ Jesus.

— 1 Thessalonians 5:18 NLT

And whatever you do or say, do it as a representative of the Lord Jesus, giving thanks through him to God the Father.

— Colossians 3:17 NLT

8. Don't be in a hurry to worry.

Stress is a killer! It will crush your creativity, and paralyse your enthusiasm. Living with stress is like trying to sprint through quicksand: the more frantic you become, the quicker you'll sink! Take time to recuperate. Learn to unwind from the stresses of each day.

> *So don't worry about tomorrow, for tomorrow will bring its own worries. Today's trouble is enough for today.*
> — Matthew 6:34 NLT

> *Give your burdens to the Lord,*
> *and he will take care of you.*
> *He will not permit the godly to slip and fall.*
> — Psalms 55:22 NLT

> *But when I am afraid,*
> *I will put my trust in you.*
> — Psalms 56:3 NLT

9. Your health is your wealth.

If you don't look after your body, your body won't look after you. A restless, busy lifestyle is no substitute for a daily exercise routine. Comfort food isn't comforting if it's killing you! Run, walk, cycle, swim or visit the gym. Take the time to invest in yourself because the value of good health is inestimable.

> *Don't you realize that your body is the temple of the Holy Spirit, who lives in you and was given to you by God? You do not belong to yourself, for God bought you with a high price. So you must honour God with your body.*
> — 1 Corinthians 6:19-20 NLT

*Beloved, I pray that you may prosper in all things and
be in health, just as your soul prospers..*
— 3 John 1:2 NKJV

*Nevertheless, the time will come when I will heal
Jerusalem's wounds and give it prosperity and true peace*
— Jeremiah 33:6 NLT

10. If God is all you have, you have all you need.

God is your supreme source: everything you will ever
receive or achieve in this life will be by and through the
grace of God. You are not at the mercy of people,
organisations, or religious institutions. Your future was
already settled in heaven before you arrived on earth.

*Every good gift and every perfect gift is from above,
and comes down from the Father of lights, with
whom there is no variation or shadow of turning.*
— James 1:17 NKJV

*By his divine power, God has given us everything we
need for living a godly life. We have received all of this
by coming to know him, the one who called us to
himself by means of his marvellous glory and excellence.*
— 2 Peter 1:3 NLT

*What shall we say about such wonderful things as
these? If God is for us, who can ever be against us?*
— Romans 8:31 NLT

11. God believes in you.

God is the only entity that truly knows you. He created
you. First, he carefully composed you from a careful cocktail

of your parents' genes, then he painstakingly fashioned you into the peculiar creature that you are now. He is pleased with His work. He has already vouched for you. He has etched His signature upon your life — you *are* the genuine article.

> *For God knew his people in advance, and he chose them to become like his Son, so that his Son would be the firstborn among many brothers and sisters. And having chosen them, he called them to come to him. And having called them, he gave them right standing with himself. And having given them right standing, he gave them his glory.*
> — Romans 8:29-30 NLT

> *I knew you before I formed you in your mother's womb. Before you were born I set you apart and appointed you as my prophet to the nations.*
> — Jeremiah 1:5 NLT

> *You saw me before I was born.*
> *Every day of my life was recorded in your book.*
> *Every moment was laid out*
> *before a single day had passed.*
> — Psalms 139:16 NLT

12. There is power in prayer

Nothing can manifest on this earth until it is settled in the heavenly realm. Some boil their blessings down to flukes, 'good karma' or lucky streaks. The truth is that when you learn to communicate effectively with God, miracles become the norm. Prayer releases new perspectives, fresh confidence, and an opportunity to connect with the divine.

The earnest prayer of a righteous person has great
power and produces wonderful results.
— James 5:16b NLT

"Lord, help!" they cried in their trouble,
and he saved them from their distress.
He calmed the storm to a whisper
and stilled the waves.
— Psalms 107:28-29 NLT

You can pray for anything, and if you have faith, you
will receive it.
— Matthew 21:22 NLT

13. Fasting is the key to advancing.

Fasting is like a parachute: it opens up a canopy of faith over you, enabling you to alight upon the safe ground of God's promises. Without a lifestyle of fasting, you will crash-land in all the wrong places and live your life like a daredevil. Fasting positions you for victories that are far-reaching.

Jesus replied, "This kind can be cast out only by prayer."
— Mark 9:29 NLT

"No, this is the kind of fasting I want:
Free those who are wrongly imprisoned;
lighten the burden of those who work for you.
Let the oppressed go free, and remove the chains that
bind people.?
— Isaiah 58:6 NLT

14. Vision + Action = Promotion.

There's an old Japanese proverb that says, '*Vision without*

action is a daydream. Action without vision is a nightmare.'
You will never capture a future you can't picture. The secret of your success lies in being able to visualise your tomorrow toady! If you can't *see* it, you'll never be able to *seize* it.

> *Indeed, the Sovereign Lord never does anything until he reveals his plans to his servants the prophets.*
> — Amos 3:7 NLT

> *This vision is for a future time.*
> *It describes the end, and it will be fulfilled.*
> *If it seems slow in coming, wait patiently,*
> *for it will surely take place.*
> *It will not be delayed.*
> — Habakkuk 2:3 NLT

15. Your mind is a goldmine.

Your mind is a miracle centre. Limitless and free, your brain can generate destiny-defining innovations and ideas. Learn to harness your imagination, and capture your thoughts clearly, using tools such as mind maps etc. Remember: if you stop thinking, you'll start sinking!

> *And be renewed in the spirit of your mind ...*
> — Ephesians 4:23 NKJV

> *And do not be conformed to this world, but be transformed by the renewing of your mind, that you may prove what is that good and acceptable and perfect will of God.*
> — Romans 12:2 NKJV

> *Call to Me, and I will answer you, and show you great and mighty things, which you do not know*
> — Jeremiah 33:3 NKJV

16. Love is life's greatest gift.

Love is acceptance. Love is self-sacrifice. Love is safety. Love is freedom to be one's self. Love is equality. Love is forgiveness. Love is mercy. Love is truthfulness. Love is patience. Filling your life with love will enrich your days, and make your years worthwhile.

> *Hatred stirs up strife,*
> *But love covers all sins.*
>
> — Proverbs 10:12 NKJV

> *Such love has no fear, because perfect love expels all fear.*
> — 1 John 4:18a NLT

> *Love never gives up, never loses faith, is always*
> *hopeful, and endures through every circumstance.*
> — 1 Corinthians 13:7 NLT

17. Matters of the heart matter.

Your heart is a treasure trove. It is the most sacred chamber of your temple. Within this inner sanctum lies the hidden jewels of your true personality. Your heart should never be a public place. It should only be accessible to those that value you, and are committed to your mental, emotional and spiritual wellbeing.

> *Guard your heart above all else,*
> *for it determines the course of your life.*
> — Proverbs 4:23 NLT

> *A good person produces good things from the treasury*
> *of a good heart, and an evil person produces evil*
> *things from the treasury of an evil heart. What you*
> *say flows from what is in your heart.*
> — Luke 6:45 NLT

18. Love your enemies but don't make yourself vulnerable to them.

Curiosity may have killed the cat, but I'm sure naivety was an accomplice! Loving your enemies doesn't guarantee that they will love you back. So forgive your enemies, pray for them and be kind to them — but never expose or entrust yourself to them. Never put yourself in harm's way. Always arm yourself with godly wisdom when you are in the presence of those that would mean you harm.

> *"Look, I am sending you out as sheep among wolves. So be as shrewd as snakes and harmless as doves.*
>
> — Matthew 10:16 NLT

> *Dear friends, do not believe everyone who claims to speak by the Spirit. You must test them to see if the spirit they have comes from God. For there are many false prophets in the world.*
>
> — 1 John 4:1 NLT

> *And whosoever shall not receive you, nor hear your words, when ye depart out of that house or city, shake off the dust of your feet.*
>
> — Matthew 10:14 NKJV

19. Pick your battles carefully.

Some battles simply aren't worth your time. These pointless skirmishes can leave you drained and too depleted to face your real battles. So don't squander valuable time and energy on trivial matters — many have had their destinies obliterated by weapons of mass distraction!

But Moses told the people, "Don't be afraid. Just stand still and watch the Lord rescue you today. The Egyptians you see today will never be seen again. The Lord himself will fight for you. Just stay calm."
— Exodus 14:13-14 NLT

He said, "Listen, all you people of Judah and Jerusalem! Listen, King Jehoshaphat! This is what the Lord says: Do not be afraid! Don't be discourage by this mighty army, for the battle is not yours, but God's.
— 2 Chronocles 20:15 NLT

Dear friends, never take revenge. Leave that to the righteous anger of God. For the Scriptures say, "I will take revenge; I will pay them back," says the Lord.
— Romans 12:19 NLT

20. Choose your friends wisely.

Your affiliations determine your aspirations. Eagles don't mate with chickens — they only couple with other eagles. Always try to surround yourself with visionary individuals who are deeply committed to seeing you maximise your potential. Someone once said, 'Hurt me with the truth but don't comfort me with a lie.' Try to nurture those friendships where open, honest conversations are the norm.

...bad company corrupts good character.
— 1 Corinthians 15:33b NLT

Walk with the wise and become wise; associate with fools and get in trouble.
— Proverbs 13:20 NLT

As iron sharpens iron, So a man sharpens the countenance of his friend.

— Proverbs 27:17 NKJV

Points To Ponder ...

- What are your 3 greatest regrets in life?
- What are your 3 greatest aspirations in life?
- Would the realisation of your present goals and aspirations go some way towards nullifying those regrets?

Prayer Time

Dear Lord, I thank you for the gift of hindsight. I also thank you for the maturity and wisdom that I've gained over the years. But Lord, having acknowledged my failings and shortcomings, please give me the grace to move on. I pray for the grace to forgive myself, the courage to start afresh, and the faith to believe that my latter will be greater than my former (Haggai 2:9). Through faith in your Word, I declare that:

- *All events in my life, happen for a reason (Romans 8:28).*
- *All events in my life are subject to God-ordained seasons (Ecclesiastes 3:1-8).*
- *All events in my life fall within a divine timeline (Revelation 1:8).*
- *All events in my life will ultimately lead to God's glory (Matthew 5:16).*

CHAPTER 16

CRY FREEDOM

Every child is an artist, the problem is staying an
artist when you grow up

– Pablo Picasso

Children never cease to amaze me. Observe them closely
and you'll see exactly what I mean.

I remember watching my youngest son Nathaniel standing
on a beach for the first time. For him, being on that beach
was like visiting another planet. His little arms shot out at
right angles to the rest of his body (transforming him into
a little African Maximus Prime) — and he just took flight!
Now just to be clear, he wasn't *actually* flying of course, but
in his mind, Nathaniel had already broken out of earth's
atmosphere. Within minutes, he must have begun to gain
altitude because all of a sudden he was running much faster,
shuddering, and blowing furious engine sounds through his
little lips.

'Er Tanta,' I called out, using his nick name, 'make sure
you don't go too close to the ...' It was too late. A huge wave
suddenly rose up and broke over his head, swallowing him
completely, and he was thrown to the ground. I came running
(but it was one of those cool runs that black men do to give
the impression that everything's still under control). But
then, I was suddenly stopped in my tracks by this strange,
squealing sound: *laughter.*

Nathaniel had been enraptured by the experience in spite of the hard facts:

- He couldn't swim.

- He didn't have a change of clothes.

- He didn't know whether or not he'd be in trouble with mummy and daddy.

- He had no prior experience of dealing with an entity as powerful as the sea.

He simply savoured the moment. He was fearless. His was a model of perfect faith: as long as Dad was somewhere there in the background, the sea was nothing but an over-grown puddle to splash in. He wasn't in the least bit shaken. Even when I reached him, trying to figure out how to dry him off, he was still giggling uncontrollably.

'Dad, did you see that?' he asked clearly delighted with himself.

'Yes son, I did.' I replied, 'what happened out there mate?'

'An alien monster tried to get me but I got away! Ha ha ha ...'

'Aren't you cold son?' I asked.

'I'm freezing dad ... can I do it again?'

I learnt a lot that day. To begin with, I learnt that you didn't need to be a NASA employee to go on space missions. But more importantly, I was reminded that life was supposed to be fun!

My son had his priorities straight: *fun came first*. Whatever else got thrown into the mix only served to heighten his enjoyment. At one point, I even caught him secretly giggling at my frustration with his wet clothes. This boy was 'schooling' me on the fine art of capturing life's precious moments. And the first module of this course was *Freedom 101*.

BROKEN SOULS

As I said earlier, children are incredible. They are free-living creatures. They haven't yet morphed into the issue-ridden, burden-toting, anxiety-stricken victims that we adults sometimes become. Some of us run the risk of becoming old before our time as a result of our worry-poisoned lifestyles.

We agonise over fears, worries, and issues until our souls become worn out with stress. That's when life becomes a chore, and each day begins to unfold like a crude game of 'running the gauntlet'. Like staggering fugitives we try to escape the booby traps of life. We duck and dive through each hour until we finally collapse into a mountain of empty beer cans, or free-fall into a valley of broken dreams.

Then something indistinct snaps within us; something we find impossible to define. Our loved ones try to help us, but can't because we've become so volatile and fragile, surrounding ourselves with a carpet of egg shells. Life becomes torture rather than an adventure. We survive rather than thrive. Our lives becomes a matter of 'endure-ment' rather than enjoyment.

As I recall my son's playful antics on the beach, I have to ask you a serious question. When was the last time that you had some fun? You know, actually squealed with excitement at some new experience? When was the last time your heart pounded with the raw anticipation of a brand new adventure? Have you forgotten how to play? Be honest.

Have you lost the gift of spontaneity? Have you forgotten how to paint masterpieces with your mind?

When the canvas of your imagination becomes so tarnished with the pressures of life that you no longer find time to dream, then it's time to cry *freedom!*

FREEDOM FIGHTERS

We escaped like a bird from a hunter's trap.
The trap is broken, and we are free!

— Psalms 124:7 NLT

Dear friend, Let me remind you of something that probably hasn't occurred to you lately. Despite the pile of bills waiting to be paid, and beyond the mountain of incomplete to-do lists strewn across your office desk, *you deserve to be happy!* In spite of those ever-mounting pressures, you are still entitled to a bit of peace and contentment in this life.

May I be frank with you? Even if you were to drive yourself into an early grave, trying to meet everyone's expectations, the world wouldn't stop spinning without you. The globe wouldn't even 'take five' in honour of all your heroic efforts to 'tick all the boxes'.

No, the hard-boiled truth, is that everything would just keep ticking along as per usual. Nothing would change in the world. Soap operas would still be spewing out the same ol' story lines; nutcases would still be blowing people up to prove how peaceful their religion is; and parents would still be agonising over the coolest way to teach their kids about the Birds and the Bees!

My point, is that *stress isn't worth it.* Stress is a harsh and ungrateful task master. The only wages one can expect from him are: ulcers, high blood pressure, strokes, heart failure — with no annual leave — and a few nervous breakdowns thrown in for the Christmas bonus!

Now, if you're living as a stress-slave today, I would like to invite you to join the *Revolution.* Become a 'freedom fighter' — and get your life back! But before you do, I must issue a little disclaimer. Your fight won't actually be against physical enemies like foreign invaders or home-grown terrorists. No. Your battles will be against unseen forces: the 'voices' in your head committed to destroying your quality of life. The Bible speaks quite clearly about this level of warfare:

> *For we are not fighting against flesh-and-blood enemies,*
> *but against evil rulers and authorities of the unseen*
> *world, against mighty powers in this dark world and*
> *against evil spirits in the heavenly places.*
> — Ephesians 6:12 NLT

Daily, you'll find yourself embroiled in a bitter war with these *voices.* They'll try to ride your brainwaves like crazy, one-eyed, pirates. First, they'll try to raid every piece of real-estate in your skull, then they'll attempt to build their wicked fortresses: frustration, depression, anger, jealousy, greed, envy, loneliness, hopelessness etc.

Now when it comes to dealing with these mind-pirates, the Bible makes it clear that conventional weapons won't work:

> *For though we walk in the flesh, we do not war according*
> *to the flesh. For the weapons of our warfare are not*
> *carnal but mighty in God for pulling down strongholds,*
> — 2 Corinthians 10:3-4 NKJV

So you can put your rocket-launchers and anti-tank missiles away ... *at least for the time being anyway.*

No, to demolish these negative forces and their fortresses, one must use subtle strategies. Time-proven tactics that will wrong-foot the enemy, and send those voices scarpering.

> *So don't go to war without wise guidance;*
> *victory depends on having many advisers.*
> — Proverbs 24:6 NLT

FROM STRESSED TO BLESSED

The following is a list of some of my favourite strategies. Feel free to try them out (or modify them) to suit your needs.

1. Write a 'have done' list.

We all get anxious at times about our ever-growing to-do lists. One of the ways to silence mind pirates is by writing a huge have-done list. Have a go at itemising all the tasks that you've completed. Referring to your have-done list frequently, will provide a ready reminder of your hard work.

> *So on October 2 the wall was finished—just fifty-two days after we had begun. When our enemies and the surrounding nations heard about it, they were frightened and humiliated. They realized this work had been done with the help of our God.*
> — Nehemiah 6:15-16 NLT

2. Write a brief synopsis of your 5 greatest lifetime achievements.

Stress often causes us to dismiss our successes, and obsess about our failures. By taking the time to write about your achievements, you may be pleasantly surprised. Once completed, place your list somewhere accessible. Reading about your achievements regularly, will encourage and inspire you.

> *But these are written so that you may continue to believe that Jesus is the Messiah, the Son of God, and that by believing in him you will have life by the power of his name.*
>
> — John 20:31 NLT

3. Make a list of all the ways you've changed in the last 5 years.

Often, we become so discouraged by our unchanging circumstances, that we fail to recognise the miracles of transformation happening in our lives. Learning to chart your changes, gives you the opportunity to appreciate how creative, adaptive and dynamic you really are.

> *So all of us who have had that veil removed can see and reflect the glory of the Lord. And the Lord—who is the Spirit—makes us more and more like him as we are changed into his glorious image.*
>
> — 2 Corinthians 3:18 NLT

4. Ask a trusted friend to make a list of all the ways that

you've changed in the last 5 years. Compare and contrast the two lists.

Sometimes in the 'heat of the battle' we become blinded by struggles and don't necessarily see all the angles. Asking a trusted friend to list the ways that you've changed/developed, can bring a much-needed freshness to your perspective.

> *Get all the advice and instruction you can,*
> *so you will be wise the rest of your life.*
> — Proverbs 19:20 NLT

5. Learn to categorise your problems.

Never put all your rotten eggs in one basket! Have you ever noticed how one rotten fruit in a fruit bowl soon contaminates the rest? Problems work in exactly the same way: rolled together into one, the burden soon becomes unbearable. Always attempt to solve one problem at a time.

> *So don't worry about tomorrow, for tomorrow will*
> *bring its own worries. Today's trouble is enough for today.*
> — Matthew 6:34 NLT

6. Keep a book of favourite sayings.

Sometimes it can be difficult to break the cycle of negative thoughts floating around in our heads (mind-pirate alert!). Something you may find useful, is keeping a compilation of your favourite sayings close to hand. These could be a collection of your favourite scriptures, lines from poems, quotes from great leaders etc. Reading something that inspires you, can be like a shot of courage to your heart,

and can provide encouragement when there's no one
else around.

> *Timely advice is lovely,*
> *like golden apples in a silver basket.*
> — Proverbs 25:11 NLT

7. Expand your emotional vocabulary.

When you are stressed out, write down all the words that
express how you feel. Learning to articulate your feelings
properly, will help you manage your relationships more
effectively. Whether at home or at work, the ability to
express your thoughts, choices and decisions clearly, will
help you establish healthy boundaries in your life.

> *The tongue can bring death or life; those who love to*
> *talk will reap the consequences.*
> — Proverbs 18:21 NLT

8. Find a secret place.

It could be a favourite bench in your local park. It could be
a much-loved walkway along a nearby river/canal. It could
be right in the middle of the busiest coffeehouse in town.
But try to find somewhere that you can retreat to and be
anonymous. Sometimes, we can only truly unwind when
we're alone.

> *After sending them home, he went up into the hills by*
> *himself to pray. Night fell while he was there alone.*
> — Matthew 14:23 NLT

9. Find a form of exercise that feels natural.

Exercise is one of nature's most effective forms of stress-relief. It reduces stress hormones like cortisol, and releases endorphins (the body's natural feel-good hormones) into the blood stream. Unfortunately, with our manic schedules, we rarely find the time to enjoy it's benefits. So, try to find a form of exercise that you really enjoy. Running, walking, cycling, swimming, even exercise DVDs at home. The more natural the exercise feels to you, the more likely you'll be to adopt it as a lifestyle.

> *Physical training is good, but training for godliness is much better, promising benefits in this life and in the life to come.*"
>
> — 1 Timothy 4:8 (emphasis mine) NLT

10. Find a new hobby.

I know, I know … it sounds too simple to take seriously. But before you dismiss it and jump to the next point, please hear me out. A hobby forces you to 'down tools', and take a break. A hobby is also like an adult form of 'play time', and helps us re-engage with our creative side.

> *Whatever your hand finds to do, do it with your might; for there is no work or device or knowledge or wisdom in the grave where you are going.*
>
> — Ecclesiastes 9:10 NKJV

11. Have a 'make over'.

Have you ever heard the expression 'power dressing' or 'dressing down'? Often, the way we dress affects how we feel, our body language, and even how we interact with others. If you walk around dressed like Mr Bean's long-lost cousin, you'll probably feel and behave like him/her. We dress up for weddings, job interviews, and other special occasions, so why not treat everyday as a 'special occasion'? Never underestimate the effect that your appearance has on your confidence?

> *Pharaoh sent for Joseph at once, and he was quickly brought from the prison. After he shaved and changed his clothes, he went in and stood before Pharaoh.*
> — Genesis 41:14 NLT

> *Before each young woman was taken to the king's bed, she was given the prescribed twelve months of beauty treatments—six months with oil of myrrh, followed by six months with special perfumes and ointments.*
> — Esther 2:12 NLT

12. Have a Spring Clean.

Before you launch head-on into your new make over, you'll need to make room for the change. This will involve getting rid of some of those old, frumpy, wish-I-could-remember-where-they-bought-me items of clothing, that are hanging around in your wardrobe like old ghosts. Please rid yourself of them. Unless they are timeless classics, they're doing nothing for your self-esteem.

> *"Do not remember the former things, Nor consider the things of old. Behold, I will do a new thing, Now it shall spring forth; Shall you not know it? I will even make a road in the wilderness And rivers in the desert.*
> — Isaiah 43:18-19 NKJV

13. Book yourself a holiday Alone.

Picture this: sand, sea, fruit cocktails, a play list of your favourite songs, and a stack of books by your favourite author. Ok, four out of five can't be bad! Perhaps you aren't in a position to fly off to the Caribbean right now, but you can still book yourself somewhere affordable for a few days. It could be a hotel, a spa, a health farm, or even a quaint little B&B somewhere off the coast. The point here is to get away on your own. You deserve a break, and I am praying that you'll find the courage and conviction to treat yourself.

> *Elijah was afraid and fled for his life. He went to Beersheba, a town in Judah, and he left his servant there.*
>
> *Then he went on alone into the wilderness, traveling all day. He sat down under a solitary broom tree and prayed that he might die. "I have had enough, Lord,"* *he said. "Take my life, for I am no better than my ancestors who have already died."*
>
> *Then he lay down and slept under the broom tree. But as he was sleeping, an angel touched him and told him, "Get up and eat!"*
>
> — 1 Kings 19:3-5 NLT

14. Learn something new.

Learning something new, is one of the most effective ways to raise your self-esteem. It will also open new doors of possibility to you, and remind you how versatile you are. If you're predominantly a 'left-brain' person (logic, lists, linearity, numbers, sequence, etc.), then why not challenge and develop your 'right-brain' functions (rhythm imagination, daydreaming, spacial awareness, etc.) and vice versa. Tackle something that draws you out of your comfort zone. Doing so will enhance your skill set as well as build your confidence.

> *A wise man will hear and increase learning, And a man of understanding will attain wise counsel ...*
> — Proverbs 1:5 NKJV

> *The wise are mightier than the strong, and those with knowledge grow stronger and stronger.*
> — Proverbs24:5 NLT

Points To Ponder ...

- Did you know that Albert Einstein is said to have stumbled upon his theory of relativity while daydreaming about riding beside a sunbeam to the edge of the universe? Or that Isaac Newton developed his theory of gravity after idly observing an apple fall from a tree? Could it be possible that some of your greatest break-through ideas and solutions, will come to you when you allow yourself the time and room to dream?

- If you suddenly inherited 3 million pounds and never had to worry about bills ever again, what would you do with your life? The answer/answers that you give, may reveal what you really *ought* to be doing with your life.

- Finances can often be one of the biggest reasons for burying one's dream/passions. What other obstacles in your life keep you from exploring new horizons?

Prayer Time

Dear Lord, thank you for this season of freedom and release in my life. I also thank you for putting everything in place that I'll ever need to acquire peace and find contentment. Lord, please help me break any cycles of stress-inducing behaviour in my life. Teach me to value each moment. Help me recapture the innocent enjoyment of the simple things in life. Renew my mind and teach me to dream again. I pray for a flood of new and exciting ideas. And finally, I pray for the courage to make changes and begin a new chapter in my life. By faith I declare that:

- *I'm breaking free from all mind traps (Psalms 124:7).*

- *I'm breaking free from all emotional blackmail (Hebrews 13:6).*

- *I'm breaking free from all insecurities (Philippians 4:13).*

- *I'm breaking free from the domain of stress (Isaiah 26:3) Amen.*

CHAPTER 17

SOUL SURVIVORS

*Experience is not what happens to you. Experience is what
you do with what happens to you.*

—Aldous Huxley

I F THERE WAS such a thing as an OBE for survival
skills, you and I would be first in line for the nomination.
My friend, you and I have endured things that would make
Bear Grylls curl up in the corner, suck his thumb, and rock
himself to sleep!

On Day 1 of our existence, we were parachute-dropped
into the deepest, darkest, forest imaginable: *The Jungle Of Life.*
Hot, humid, and frightening, this new environment teemed
with threats on every side.

We weren't informed about the family we would be born
to. We weren't consulted about our ethnicity, neither were we
invited to any negotiations about the part of the globe we'd
be landing on.

No. We were simply jettisoned from the womb and
suddenly found ourselves free-falling into the creepy abyss
of life. We had no map, no compass, and no survival manual.
We didn't even have any Rafiki-looking tribesman at our side
singing weird songs about squashed bananas (*The Lion King*).

So we did our best. We took the only items in our rucksacks
(God's grace and some razor-sharp instincts), and just forged
our way ahead.

But it wasn't easy. Along the way, we wrestled with pythons: soul-crushing situations that tried to choke the hope out of us. We battled with fevers: melancholy atmospheres that filled us with fear and left us in a cold sweat about the future. There were times when we were covered in leeches too: people in our lives whose only motive was to take, take, take. And we were constantly molested by creatures of the night: visitors from the underworld that picked up our scent by day and hunted us in the night like prey.

NEEDS MUST WHEN THE DEVIL DRIVES

But we survived. How? We learnt the 'law of the jungle'. We became creatures of instinct, and adapted to our environments. Our eyes adjusted to the darkness: the lies; the greed; the cheating; the propaganda; the betrayal.

Our ears became attuned to the shrill mating calls of false lovers: those who would use us, abuse us, and then try to loose us.

We learnt that there was strength in numbers, so we moved in packs: social cliques that allowed us in — as long as we never forgot 'our place'.

But perhaps our greatest accomplishment in the jungle was mastery of the most subtle of all survival skills: camouflage. We learnt to blend in perfectly with the foliage: corrupt administrations; lying institutions; oppressive traditions. Like hybrid chameleons, we morphed and shape-shifted our way through life.

LOST

On one level, I suppose we're to be congratulated. Our survival in life's jungle to this point, testifies of our incredible resilience. You and I are warriors … *Spartans*. And whilst I am thankful for the survival skills we picked up along the way, it must be said that jungle life is only fine for a time. After a while, your nerves start to fray at the edges.

You see, in the jungle, you can run but all your hiding places are the abode of vipers. Safety is a delusion. How do you domesticate creatures who salivate at the very sight of you? No. True success can only come to those who make it out of there.

So, some try tunnelling their way out. They turn their backs on 'the norm' and try to forge out new ways of living. Alternative lifestyles. They dislocate their souls and pray that if a million and one new laws get passed through parliament, perhaps what they do will eventually start to feel natural.

Some try blasting their way out. They join terror groups: fascists in fancy dress. They calmly strap bombs to their chests and blow themselves to smithereens in the hope that the next life will be better than the present one.

Some try floating out. They try to escape from 'the jungle' without physically leaving it. Inspired by all the greenery around them, they soon start smoking it! If religion is the opium of the masses, then marijuana must be the communion wafer of the bored, and the stupid. High on whatever substance they can get their hands on: coke, charlie, boppers, poppers, jiggas, stackers, beanies, skunk, joy juice, they take make-believe trips out of the jungle. But the sad reality, is that no matter how high they get, they never quite leave the jungle floor let alone soar free above its canopy.

BYE BYE LITTLE ROBIN

Now, please don't get me wrong. I'm not perched on some soapbox pontificating about how people ought to live their lives. Free will is heaven's greatest 'Bill of Rights'. The only reason why I am speaking so plainly about life on the jungle floor, is because I was trapped there for the best part of 22 years. And believe me when I say that I tried *everything* that I could think of to break loose.

My time in the jungle wasn't exactly the kind of romantic tale that Disney would want to adopt. Trust me when I say that I was no Mowgli (*The Jungle Book*). I didn't swing deftly from tree to tree communicating happily with the 'wildlife' either. No. After 22 years of trying to hack my way through the impossible, impassible foliage of life, I got my posterior unceremoniously wedged in quicksand!

It was a sinister little place in life where the more I tried to break free, the deeper I sunk in the mire of my own misery. At the time of writing this chapter, Robin Williams has just died. Suicide is a merciless spectre. It's one of those mind-pirates that has managed to pluck some of the most beautiful souls from this world. When I awoke to the news about Robin, I wept like a baby. It was too close for comfort. It was a jarring reminder of my 'swamp days.' The days when I was neck-deep in the quicksand of my own emotional anguish. The days when I had no one around to hear my cry let alone throw me a lifeline. I'll never forget it. I felt as though I was being buried alive. So I did the only thing that I had the energy left to do: I gave up. I let myself sink lower and lower.

Lower still ...

But just as I was about to blackout, I saw something strange in the distance. Through the haze of my confusion, I saw a tree. Nothing unusual there: I'm in the jungle right? But this tree was rugged and cross-shaped. And someone was impaled on it. He was bleeding and dying, and yet He still looked at me with such compassion. It was the perfect paradox: He was dying on a cross — and yet here He was, offering to save my life! The conversation:

Jesus - Mike, I died on this cross so that you wouldn't have to perish in that pit. I know you're tired, confused, and afraid but I'll make a deal with you. I'll rescue you, clean you up, and air-lift you to safety. I'll heal you of all your wounds, arm you for jungle warfare, and bring you back here to rescue others.

Michael - Ok, so what's the catch? I mean, what will I have to do to qualify for all that?

Jesus - Repent and be baptised. Ask for my help. I never go where I'm not wanted (Mark 2:17). That's what it means to be 'Born Again' Mike. It's the place where you end and I begin.

Silence ...

Michael - Get me out of this pit Lord ... and I'll serve you for the rest of my days.

❧

Dear friend, success without peace of mind is a fallacy. What good is a diamond-studded bed when you can't sleep at night? Or, what good is a portfolio full of properties when your soul is bankrupt? Success is a status only ascribed to those who have managed to escape the clutches of 'The Jungle'. But more about that in the next chapter. For now, I'd like to conclude this section by sharing 4 fascinating facts about depression in the Bible.

1. Some of the greatest figures in the bible struggled with depression.

Then he (Elijah) went on alone into the wilderness, traveling all day. He sat down under a solitary broom tree and prayed that he might die. "I have had enough, Lord," he said. "Take my life, for I am no better than my ancestors who have already died."
(1 Kings 19:4 emphasis mine NLT)

2. God is close to those who are on the brink.

The Lord is close to the brokenhearted; he rescues those whose spirits are crushed. (Psalms 34:18 NLT)

3. God will stop at nothing to save the lost.

"If a man has a hundred sheep and one of them wanders away, what will he do? Won't he leave the ninety-nine others on the hills and go out to search for the one that is lost? (Matthew 18:12 NLT)

4. The only way to move heaven on your behalf, is to call upon the lord for help.

But in my distress I cried out to the Lord; yes, I prayed to my God for help. He heard me from his sanctuary; my cry to him reached his ears. Then the earth quaked and trembled. The foundations of the mountains shook; they quaked because of his anger.
(Psalms 18: 6-7 NLT)

Points To Ponder ...

- Remember that game we played as kids where we'd have to choose what kind of animal we would be if given the chance? Well, this is the remixed version of that game. In the 'jungle of life', what kind of animal are you? Are you a predator or are you prey? What animal best describes your status in the 'food chain' of life?

- Write down the top 5 survival mechanisms that you've adopted over the years to protect yourself from life's challenges.

- In my hopelessness, I made a deal with the Lord. In exchange for my rescue, I would serve Him for the rest of my life. What would you offer the Lord in exchange for a complete turnaround in your life today?

Prayer Time

Dear Lord, thank you for always being there: I can approach your throne at anytime (Hebrews 4:16). Thank you for keeping and sustaining me through all the dangers that I've faced so far in life. I confess that I would never have made it this far without you. Your love and grace are the secrets of my survival. Lord, I'll make a deal with you today. Rescue me, and I'll rescue others. Bless me, and I'll bless others. Reveal my purpose to me, and I'll pursue it with all my heart. By faith, I now declare that:

- *My current crisis is only temporary (Psalms 34:19).*
- *My current challenges are making me stronger/wiser (Romans 8:32).*
- *Although it may not feel like it, I am never alone (Hebrews 13:5).*
- *I have divine protection (Psalms 34:7).*

CHAPTER **18**

SUCCESS 101

Success is liking yourself, liking what you do,
and liking how you do it.

– Maya Angelou

HOW WOULD YOU define success? Please don't answer impulsively. I encourage you to take a moment to reflect, before settling on your final answer. You see, your final answer will determine *everything*.

Imagine a seamstress who sets out to make the perfect wedding dress for the very first time. She searches tirelessly for the right sewing pattern, but in the end, can only get her hands on a pattern for an old nun's habit! Now, no matter how hard she labours over that dress, it's unlikely that she'll produce the wedding dress of every girl's dream. Following a pattern for a nun's habit will produce a result that'll be disappointing at best — disastrous at worst.

And how about the novice chef who decides to prepare the perfect paella? He throws himself headlong into the task, only to discover (when it's too late) that he'd accidentally followed the recipe for a Bombay curry! Now, no matter how loudly all you curry fans out there may applaud our blushing chef, the fact remains that he has utterly failed in his quest to produce a paella dish.

Similarly, the pattern of success that you carry around in your mind, will determine what you pursue in this life.

It will determine who you become, and ultimately what you will be remembered for when you are no longer here.

CAPTURE A PICTURE OF THE FUTURE

So, when you close your eyes and try to visualize a successful future for yourself, what do you see? What does success look like in your mind? What will be *your* marker for success? At what point will you allow yourself to be rewarded with heaven's greatest accolades: peace and contentment?

Will it be the day you walk down the aisle and stand at the altar of marriage? Will it be the day that you can whip out slick studio-style photographs of your 2.4 children at a school reunion? Maybe you're waiting for the day that your bank balance reaches an eyebrow-raising figure. What will it take — in your mind's eye — to feel that you've 'made it' in life? An endless stream of doting admirers? An interview with *Time* magazine? How will you know when you've made it?

The sad reality is that in my lifetime, I've been privileged to meet many individuals who have achieved some, or all of the above, and yet still remain crippled by a haunting sense of failure.

I've read about celebrities (and I'm sure you have too) that have received CBEs, MBEs and OBEs one year, and then have been booked into rehab the next! I mean, we're constantly bombarded with endless tales of divorce battles amongst tinsel towns finest. We sit and watch fascinated, as the unwitting victims of these battles (their children) are thrown into a media circus that turns them into coke-snorting, sex tape-leaking, publicity-seeking spectacles. And why? All in pursuit of that mythical, whimsical, social nirvana that people try to pass off as success.

But how do *you* define success? Those that never fully resolve this question in their minds, seldom find contentment let alone happiness. They become riddled with chronic insecurities, limping along in life like maimed veteran soldiers from a war no one cares to remember.

UNSUCCESSFUL SUCCESS

Most people's definition of success would probably look something like this:

> **THE PROGRESSIVE REALISATION OF SET GOALS AND OBJECTIVES.**

Now in an ideal world, this definition would probably suffice. But what happens when the set goals and objectives are sinister, twisted or evil? Osama Bin Laden had a set goal and a plain objective. He wanted to blow people up whilst proclaiming to the world (with a straight face) that he was doing this to make the world a better place. Hopefully you've already spotted the flaw in this generally accepted definition of success.

Although Mr. Bin Laden was able to accomplish his set goals and objectives, it would be absurd to suggest that his life on earth was a success, by any standards.

And what about the drug dealer who pulls up to the gates

of his mansion, in his brand new Mercedes-Benz S-class? He too has progressively realized all of his set goals and objectives. Unfortunately, his 'success' has meant poisoning a community with crack cocaine!

Whilst he smugly pops his feet up in his MTV Cribs-style mansion, watching his swelling bank balance via internet banking, someone, somewhere, is burying a loved one because of all of his 'accomplishments'. Some woman somewhere, is having her children taken away from her by Social Services because between her drug habit, and her prostitute-lifestyle to support it, her children have become invisible to her.

Mr. Bin Laden, and our Scar-face wannabe, have just helped us establish one very important fact. It *is* possible to succeed at doing the wrong thing. And success at doing the wrong thing, is equal to failure!

Consider this portion of scripture:

> *Then he told them a story: "A rich man had a fertile farm that produced fine crops.*
>
> *He said to himself, 'What should I do? I don't have room for all my crops.'*
>
> *Then he said, 'I know! I'll tear down my barns and build bigger ones. Then I'll have room enough to store all my wheat and other goods.*
>
> *And I'll sit back and say to myself, "My friend, you have enough stored away for years to come. Now take it easy! Eat, drink, and be merry!"'*
>
> *"But God said to him, 'You fool! You will die this very night. Then who will get everything you worked for?'*

> *"Yes, a person is a fool to store up earthly wealth but not have a rich relationship with God."*
>
> — Luke 12:16-21 NLT

The man in this parable is trapped in a tragedy: *he's a roaring success in his own eyes, but a pitiful failure in God's eyes!* He is celebrated in the eyes of men for his status, but barely tolerated in heaven for his spiritual irrelevance on earth.

THE CURSE OF BEING OFF COURSE

Imagine a man travelling to Scotland from Birmingham in the West Midlands. He joins the M6 but instead of heading north, he begins to journey south in completely the opposite direction.

No matter how fast he drives, he will never arrive at the correct destination. Even if onlookers along the way are bowled-over by his Lamborghini Huracan, ultimately, his journey has failed. His journey is unsuccessful because he will never arrive in Scotland by travelling south.

Likewise, it isn't how quickly an individual appears to be progressing in life that counts, but whether or not they are travelling in the right direction.

Being off course in life, is like being trapped in a curse. Imagine reaching the end of your days and suddenly realising that everything you did had been in the opposite direction of your purpose. On closer examination, you realise that:

- Your relationships were off course.
- Your investments were off course.
- Your career choices were off course.

- Your decisions, choices and outcomes were off course.
- Your prayers, prophesies and pursuits were off course.

Imagine arriving in heaven, and finding out that you spent your time on earth walking in completely the opposite direction to God's plan for your life.

For me, the only kind of success worth pursuing then, is the kind that lands you in the lap of your destiny. The kind that has you doing precisely what you were placed on this earth to do. As a pastor and counsellor of over twenty years, I've come to realise a few things. Depression and other stress-related conditions, are often borne out of fruitless pursuits. There is nothing more soul-crushing than throwing yourself headlong into the wrong things and having nothing to show for it at the end of the day. An individual can only fall flat on their face so many times before they eventually decide to remain there!

Hope deferred makes the heart sick,
but a dream fulfilled is a tree of life.
— Proverbs 13:12 NLT

SUCCESS THAT SUCCEEDS

So, as we bring this chapter to a close, let us re-define success using God's Word. According to scripture, true success is:

1. Finding, following and fulfilling God's plan and purpose for your life.

Don't copy the behavior and customs of this world, but let God transform you into a new person by changing the way you think.

Then you will learn to know God's will for you, which is good and pleasing and perfect (Romans 12:2 emphasis mine NLT)

2. Building your goals and strategies according to divine design.

Unless the Lord builds the house, They labor in vain who build it; Unless the Lord guards the city, The watchman stays awake in vain. (Psalm 127:1 NKJV).

3. Understanding your role in life and playing it to the best of your ability.

*Jesus answered, "You say rightly that I am a king. **For this cause I was born, and for this cause I have come into the world**, that I should bear witness to the truth. Everyone who is of the truth hears My voice."* (John 18:37 emphasis mine NKJV).

4. Mastering the art of being you, and becoming comfortable in your own skin.

David put it on, strapped the sword over it, and took a step or two to see what it was like, for he had never worn such things before. "I can't go in these," he protested to Saul. "I'm not used to them." So David took them off again (1 Samuel 17:39 NLT).

5. Becoming all that God intended you to become, and completing your assignment on earth.

...for after David had served his generation according to the will of God, he died...(Acts 13:36 TLB).

Points To Ponder ...

- Have you ever laboured to accomplish something believing that it would really hit the 'success gong' for you, only to be left with a ringing sense of emptiness at the end of your 'success'?

- Where did your model of success come from? Have you ever had unhealthy or unsound models of success in your life? Have any of these ever subtly crept into your way of thinking?

- How many people do you have around you that serve as ideal role-models for where you want to be in life?

Prayer Time

Dear Lord, thank you for this opportunity to prayerfully reflect on what really makes me tick. Holy Spirit I open my heart to you now. Please search and examine my motives, pursuits and desires. Holy Spirit, I ask you now to release me from fruitless pursuits. I ask you to rid my mind of any erroneous, self-harming notions of success that I may have picked up along the way. As I align my thinking with your Word, I now declare that:

- *My perspectives are being renewed (Romans 12:2).*

- *My pursuits are being reviewed (Proverbs 16:9).*

- *My passions are being refined (Psalms 139:23-24).*

- *My purpose is being revived (Proverbs 24:16) Amen.*

CHAPTER 19

GOD'S GIFT

Your talent is God's gift to you. What you do with
it is your gift back to God.

– Leo Buscaglia

THE FIRST TIME she appears on our screens, we don't
quite know what to make of her. Perhaps it's the walk.
Hers is one of those walks that suggests she might be one
sandwich short of a picnic.

When asked her name and where she's from, she answers
clearly, and without difficulty. But when the head judge
inquires about her age, she unexpectedly announces: 'I'm
47 ... and that's just one side of me!' This last comment is
punctuated with a hula-hoop motion with her hips — and
an enthusiastic pelvic thrust at the end of it.

By now, the opinion of the audience is already divided:
some are sniggering, some are cringing. And when the head
judge asks about her aspirations and who she wants to be
compared to, he rolls his eyes at her answer.

'Elaine Paige', she boldly states into the microphone. The
camera pans over the audience once more. Most of the faces
are wearing the same quizzical expression: *why do people do
these things to themselves?*

So, with a begrudging nod and a final sigh, the head judge
signals for the audition to begin. He knows as judges they

must be fair, but it's been a long day, and this is the last thing he needs.

When the first few bars of the song's intro begins, the contestant has the look of someone about to walk 'the green mile'. And then, just like that — it happens ...

I dreamed a dream in time gone by ...

When hope was high ...

And life worth living ...

Susan Magdalane Boyle (Subo), goes on to give us one of the greatest moments in British television history. Standing humbly on stage, she unveils her God-given talent to the world, and releases everything she's got into that microphone. Her mezzo-soprano voice is startling. The camera zooms in on the judges. Tears are pooling in Piers Morgan's eyes. Amanda Holden's jaw has dropped in astonishment, and Simon Cowell's eyes have begun to sparkle with pound signs!

By the time she reaches the second verse, the audience are already on their feet.

I dreamed that love would never die ...

I dreamed that God would be forgiving ...

Subo 'dreamed a dream', and on the 11th of April 2009, that dream came true. Her first album (*I Dreamed a Dream*)

was released in November of that year and instantly became the UK's best-selling debut album of all time. It even ousted previous record holder (Leona Lewis) from the top spot.

In her first year of fame, SuBo made £5 million (yes, you heard me right!). She has since performed duets with her heroes Elaine Paige and Donny Osmond, and was invited to sing at Windsor Castle for the Queen's Diamond Jubilee Pageant.

Subo didn't win Britain's Got Talent that year, she ended up in second place to the formidable dance troupe Diversity. But who cares right? Susan Boyle won something far more prestigious that day: **the knowledge of her place in this world.**

❦

In a parallel universe Susan Boyle might have been sitting in her rented accommodation in Blackburn, Scotland. She might have been curled up on a sofa — one that had seen better days — stroking Pebbles (her pet cat) and wondering:

(a) How to rid the room of the stale smell of yesterday's fish and chips

(b) Whether fish and chips two nights in a row would be too flashy.

Perhaps one of her hands would have been rummaging down the side of the sofa cushions trying to find loose change so that she could 'live dangerously' and splash out on a pot of curry sauce (Ooooo!!!).

But instead, today she's busy rubbing shoulders with the likes of Oprah Winfrey and her ilk. She's now an ambassador for Save the Children UK, and she's a committed Christian and philanthropist too (just thought I'd throw that one in there ...).

Now I don't know if it's just me, but all this begs the following questions:

- How many Subos are there out there?
- How many individuals are hiding gifts and talents that could transform their lives?

But perhaps the most important question of all is:

- Are *you* one of those individuals?

Is it possible that buried beneath your mundane existence (pardon my bluntness), lies a formidable gift? Something neatly packaged into your personality, and sealed in a place where no one would think to look? Something that you've always known was there, but were too afraid to reveal to the cynical audiences around you? Something that's been beating on the inside of you like the ultrasound of something that desperately needs to be birthed?

SUBO SEASONS

Brothers and sisters, *this is your Subo season.* It's time to step out onto life's podium, and bravely make your way towards that spotlight.

Even if they think you're one slice short of a loaf, just keep walking. Don't stop until you're right beneath that bright beam of light. Ignore the chuckles that your aspirations draw from your critics. Don't be put off by those who would judge you before they've even heard you. And don't squander too much time and energy trying to talk your would-be judges into liking you. Just wait for that sacred moment in life when the laughter finally fades and there's nothing else the crowd can do, but just let you have your moment.

That's when you've got to do it.

Close your eyes, step right up to the edge of that precipice, and take a leap of faith into your destiny. Give it all you've got my friend. Release everything you have; everything you are; and everything that you ever hope to be into that single magical moment. The Lord is by your side. The Holy Spirit will be the wind beneath your wings. By the time you open your eyes again, you'll be airborne! Do it now! Stun your generation, and transform your life. Your gift can open doors for you that will defy the imagination:

> *A man's gift makes room for him,*
> *And brings him before great men.*
>
> — Proverbs 18:16 NKJV

X FACTOR

Finding your area of excellence can be tough though. And people won't always be quick to appreciate, let alone celebrate your abilities. Sometimes — depending on factors such as your family background, your cultural heritage, the school you attended etc. — your gift can be missed or ignored altogether. This is partly because of earlier traditions within the education community.

At the beginning of the 20th century, a French psychologist called Alfred Binet, came up with a series of Intelligence Quotient (IQ) tests. These tests were based purely on verbal and numeric abilities, and were accepted without question for over 60 years. But in the 1980s, a professor at Harvard University (Howard Gardner) began to uncover something known as the theory of multiple intelligence.

Gardner's research was extensive. It involved tests, interviews, and a study of a wide spectrum of individuals: stroke and accident victims, prodigies, autistic individuals, those with learning difficulties, and people from diverse cultures. What Gardner found was staggering. He postulated that the traditional notion of intelligence (and giftedness) based on IQ testing was very limited. He concluded from his findings that:

'Intelligence is the ability to find and solve problems, and create products of value in one's own culture.'
— Howard Gardner

Since then, others like Robert Ornstein and Tony Buzan have helped reform and redefine practices within education communities around the world. Instead of recognising only two areas of gifting in people — verbal and numerical — educators are now also turning their attention to many other kinds of intelligences and abilities.

The reason for this brief history lesson (and I hope I haven't lost you) was to prompt the following questions:

- Was the system that you grew up in bias/ignorant about multiple intelligences?

- Did your teachers/parents ignore or dismiss your area of intelligence?

- If so, did their response cause you to 'shelve' any of these abilities?

Susan Boyle was 47 before the world took note of her incredible gift. Perhaps you can be spared years of wasted opportunities by learning to identify where you are most 'intelligent'. The following is a list of these intelligences, with a brief description of each. Take note of the ones that resonate with you particularly, as these may be pointing you in the direction of your 'X factor'.

1. Verbal Intelligence
Those that possess this intelligence are 'wordsmiths'. Words thrill them. They delight in taking the 26 letters of the alphabet, and flinging them together in creative ways. They can paint pictures with their words, and convey ideas and insights in clear and creative ways. They are life's natural communicators.

2. Numeric Intelligence
Wait a minute! Before you quickly skip to the next point, consider the following: this intelligence isn't just about solving mathematical problems. Those that are gifted in this area, also have a flare for patterns, systems, and chains of reasoning. They relish the challenge of problem solving. They are curious individuals who love to investigate, experiment and test how things work.

3. Spatial Intelligence

This is the lowest of all my intelligences. The Lord had to give me a wife highly gifted in this area to compensate for its virtual absence in my life. Spatial intelligence enables you to navigate and negotiate your surroundings successfully. These guys are brilliant with maps (I love you Katrina), jigsaw puzzles, 3-D modelling, charts etc. They give us our architects, formula One drivers, gymnasts, footballers, sky-divers etc.

4. Creative Intelligence

These guys are gifted with originality. They think in new ways and as a result, sometimes get in trouble with authority. Creative intelligence gives us our business entrepreneurs, inventors, musicians, teachers, film makers, graphic designers etc. Those blessed with this intelligence make our world more colourful.

5. Musical Intelligence

Those with this intelligence are especially sensitive to sound and rhythm. They hear the rhythms and melodies of life, as it were, and turn them into musical expressions. They play instruments, sing, dance or hum their way through the storms of life. Their passion for music is infectious and their tastes cover a huge spectrum of styles.

6. Kinesthetic (physical) Intelligence

Those blessed with this intelligence annoyed us the most

at school. They are naturally brilliant at every sport. They are physically co-ordinated, poised and well balanced. They can do amazing things with their bodies. Their body language is eloquent, and they give us our actors, surgeons, sports stars, dancers etc.

7. Intrapersonal (personal) Intelligence

This is perhaps one of the most underestimated of all the intelligences. Those gifted in this area are completely comfortable in their own skins. They've been endowed with a deep understanding of what makes them tick, and they are 'at peace' with themselves. They know how to process their personal experiences, and overcome personal adversity without the need for 'drama'. They enjoy their own company, and are always searching for new ways to improve and develop themselves. Those blessed with this intelligence give us our artists, writers, life-coaches, positive thinkers, reformers etc.

8. Interpersonal (social) Intelligence

Those gifted in this area interact with others effortlessly. They find it easy to empathise with others, and can communicate almost intuitively. They appreciate and accommodate different kinds of people, and can make quick, on-the-spot adjustments within themselves to put others at ease. These give us our public speakers, playwrights, political leaders etc.

9. Spiritual Intelligence.

Those gifted in this area seem superhuman. They are blessed with a global vision, and can see far beyond their own interests. They are compassionate, God-conscious, and are motivated by the well-being of others. This intelligence gives us people like Mother Teresa, Martin Luther King, Florence Nightingale etc. They are courageous, influential and visionary.

Points To Ponder ...

- Some win gold medals at the Olympics. Some win world championships. Some win competitions like Britain's Got Talent, and My Kitchen Rules. If you had the opportunity to showcase a single gift on the world's stage, what would it be?
- On a scale of 1-10, how ready are you to showcase this gift?
- Write down 10 ways that you can develop and sharpen this gift.

Prayer Time

Dear Lord, thank you for the many talents that I have been blessed with. I realise now that I have a treasury of unused gifts and a reservoir of untapped potential. I ask that you designate this season of my life as a time of discovery. Help me discover, develop, and deploy all of my gifts. Employ them for your plan and purpose. Help me become an asset to my generation. Anoint me to make my debut in the spirit realm (Acts 19:15). Release a radiance in my life. Break every deadlock and stalemate in my life.

By faith, I now declare that:

- *This is my season to shine (Psalms 102:13, Isaiah 60:1).*

- *Those who ridiculed me in the past will celebrate me at last (Luke 20:17).*

- *My gifts will open up new doors of opportunity for me (Proverbs 18:16).*

- *I am anointed to overcome the opposition that these opportunities attract (1 Corinthians 16:9).*

CHAPTER 20

ON YOUR MARKS

If it doesn't challenge you, it doesn't change you.

– Fred DeVito

G ET SET ... WAIT!!! It's nearly time for lift-off, but before you hit the launch button — there's just one more thing that we need to discuss. By now you've possibly got a clearer picture of where you'd like to be in life. If you're like me, then once a seed of an idea germinates in your mind, an entire orchard of possibilities soon comes into full bloom. Perhaps for the first time in a long while, you feel a fresh precipitation of prospects washing over you. I'm excited for you! I feel as if I've been blessed with Royal-Box tickets to the premier your emergence. My dear friend it's been an honour travelling with you through the pages of this book. Thank you for investing your time and thoughts in this journey.

As we approach the last part of this book, I'd like to leave you with a final challenge. Consider the following questions:

- Why do some people do better than others?

- Why do some people attain academic qualifications while others quit and develop a phobia for studies?

- How is it that some transform themselves into athletes while others completely let themselves go?

- Why are some folks wealthy while others are barely able to rub two pennies together?

- If a person is *doing* better than you, does that mean that they *are* better than you?

The first 4 questions are rhetorical — you don' t have to answer them right now. You can simply reflect on them, and unpack them later. The fifth question however, is worth dealing with now.

Most people who succeed in life do so because they've picked up a few cutting-edge principles along the way. This may be through their family backgrounds, their education, or through their associations. I'd like to leave you with 5 practical pointers and winning strategies that I can recommend. Now the Bible teaches that:

> History merely repeats itself. It has all been done before. Nothing under the sun is truly new.
>
> Ecclesiastes 1:9 NLT

The principals that I'm about to share with you aren't new by any means, but I'm hoping that they'll serve as useful prompts and reminders to help you approach your goals more pragmatically.

YOUR A-GAME

1. The principle of planning on paper.
Always commit your plans, strategies and ideas to paper. Whether you choose to scribble your ideas on a note pad,

sketch a mind map on an old piece of tissue paper, or record your ideas on a recording device, always try to capture your ideas in a tangible form. Someone once asked Thomas Edison how he managed to give the world so many inventions. His reply was: 'Because I never think in words, I think in pictures.'

Inspired moments are like clouds: they're constantly moving, evolving and taking on new shapes. Like an artist taking advantage of a beautiful landscape, always be prepared to capture what you see in your mind's eye, and translate it into a form that you can refer back to later on.

2. The principle of ordered priorities.

Once you've captured your plans, goals and objectives on paper, the next step will be making a list of all that you'll have to do to achieve them. List them in order from the simplest, to the most gruelling tasks. Try to arrange them in order of priorities.

Make a start wherever feels most comfortable, but try to tick something off your list each day/week (depending on what it is). Remember, in an average day, you can't do everything, but you can definitely do *something*.

3. The principle of preparation.

Upgrade yourself! Even when the company, Apple, receives bad press about one of its products (like phones that love limbo dancing!) it can still boast of queues a mile long each time their doors open to release a new product. Why? It's because Apple is committed to upgrading its products in any and every way imaginable.

Always aim to be better next year than you are this year. Book yourself on one-day courses, seminars, conferences etc. Aim to become a much sought-after authority in your field. Amidst this awesome technological age, where information is available to us at the click of a button, there is absolutely no excuse for ignorance!

4. The principle of pressure.
In this book I've talked a lot about lifting-off, so let's take a closer look at the 'rocket' principle and how it works.

In order for a rocket to be successfully launched out of earth's orbit, a tremendous amount of pressure is required. By mixing a fuel (like hydrogen) with an oxidizer (like liquid oxygen), something tantamount to an explosion occurs in the combustion chamber, sending the rocket hurtling into space. That's the power of pressure folks!

I don't know about you, but I sometimes work best under pressure. Harnessed and channelled properly, pressure can sometimes be a brilliant motivator.

5. The principle of productivity.
For years, the enemy tormented me with the fear that I'd never have children. It was a random and ridiculous fear, nevertheless, it was relentless. But the first time I held my eldest son Joshua in my arms, the enemy's case collapsed like a house of cards. After my second son, well, lets just say that I never had to entertain the thought ever again. Likewise, there is nothing that encourages the heart and imbues one with confidence like 'bearing fruit'.

Once you start seeing the fruit of your labours, the way you see yourself will change. In your mind, you'll go from dreamer to visionary in a heartbeat.

Points To Ponder ...

- How much do you believe in your vision/dream?
- If a multi-millionaire like Alan Sugar or Richard Branson was willing to sponsor your vision, what would be the first thing you'd need to put in place?
- Write down 3 major ways that your life would change as a result of your vision coming to pass.

Prayer Time

Heavenly Father, thank you for bringing me to such a wonderful place in my life. You have been so gracious to me. You have blessed me with so many opportunities to be productive, and I vow to start putting my time to better use. Your Word confirms that it's your will for be to be fruitful (John 15:5), and I pray for the resolve and will power to be more disciplined with my time.

By faith, I now declare that:

- *I will receive innovative ideas from the Lord (Deuteronomy 8:18).*
- *I will receive cutting-edge strategies from heaven (Genesis 41:32-37).*
- *I will learn to be more organised, and I will synchronise my life with heaven's timetable (Mark 6:39-40).*
- *I am now operating with the spirit of excellence (Proverbs 17:27) Amen.*

COMING SOON:

ASPIRE

Treat Yourself To The Truth

IF ONLY I knew *then* what I know now! How many times have we uttered that statement over the years? Who amongst us hasn't fantasized about travelling back in time and dealing with a situation differently?

Arguments. Destructive relationships. Awful decisions. Unjust outcomes. Oh how we'd love to re-visit those times armed with the knowledge, experience, and wisdom that we have now!

But what if we could serve up those lashings of wisdom in **real time**? What if from now on, we were able to deal with every-day dilemmas armed with time-proven wisdom keys?

In his next title: ASPIRE (Treat Yourself To The Truth), Michael Ekwulugo shares a hundred and one time-proven truths that every aspiring visionary **must** be armed with in order to fulfil their life's calling.

At a time when institutionalised political correctness threatens the very foundations of our belief system, this timely book comes as a much-needed breath of fresh air!

For more information, please connect with Michael at:

www.ekwministries.co.uk